ONE BY ONE

ONE BY ONE

DAVID A. BEDNAR

DESERET
BOOK

SALT LAKE CITY, UTAH

Library of Congress Cataloging-in-Publication Data
(CIP on file)
ISBN 978-1-62972-382-2

Printed in the United States of America
Lake Book Manufacturing, Inc., Melrose Park, IL

10   9   8   7   6   5   4   3   2

CONTENTS

ONE BY ONE AND SPIRITUAL PATTERNS

The first experience I had on an assignment as a member of the Quorum of the Twelve Apostles of The Church of Jesus Christ of Latter-day Saints occurred on the weekend following my call to serve, my sustaining in general conference, and my ordination and setting apart. I traveled to a city in the United States to preside at a stake conference and was greeted at the airport by the stake president. As he and I were driving from the airport to the stake center and talking about the conference, I asked him the following question, "President, why do you think the Lord sent the newest member of the Twelve to your stake this weekend?"

He responded, "I really have no idea."

I then said, "Well, I do not know either. I am new at this. I believe you will know the answer to that question before I do. So, just as soon as you figure it out, please let me know."

We were approximately halfway to the stake center when the president turned to me and said, "Elder Bednar, I think I may know one of the reasons why the Lord sent you to this stake this weekend."

I requested, "Please, tell me."

He explained, "I have a brother who joined the Church five years ago. He is struggling with a specific challenge. Would you be willing to visit with him?"

I replied, "I would be happy to."

An appointment was arranged, and after the Saturday evening session of conference I went to the high council room, where the stake president's brother was waiting for me. I entered the room having given no prior thought to what I would say or do. The man stood up. I greeted him and shook his hand. I introduced myself and said, "Two days ago I was ordained and set apart to be an authorized representative of the Lord Jesus Christ. And the Savior sent me to this stake this weekend to deliver a specific message to you: You can do this. As His servant, I promise you will have His help to face this challenge and overcome it."

I embraced him. We talked for several minutes. I gave the man my contact information and invited him to update me periodically about his progress. We walked together out of the high council room after a brief but edifying experience.

The stake president may have believed that this divinely orchestrated encounter was intended primarily to bless and benefit his brother. But as I reflected repeatedly on this experience, I realized the Lord had provided me with one of the most impactful learning opportunities I could ever receive. I had been sent to represent and speak for the Lord in delivering a message to the stake president's brother. And the method of delivery was *one by one.*

A SPIRITUAL PATTERN

People frequently ask me to identify and share some of the important lessons I have learned during my years of service as a member of the Quorum of the Twelve. Because I am blessed to meet, serve with, and learn from faithful Church members all over the world, the lessons are many and wide-ranging. Over the years, however, the principle and spiritual pattern of *one by one* has blessed me and influenced my ministry in powerful ways. This book is an attempt to describe that basic truth and some of its implications for each of us.

The life and ministry of the Lord Jesus Christ are the greatest examples of the principle of *one by one.* I believe the scriptural phrase *one by one* (1) reveals essential aspects of what we need to know about and emulate in the Savior's nature, attributes, and character and (2) teaches us in powerful ways how we are to minister to and serve God's children.

Elder Joseph B. Wirthlin taught this truth: "True disciples of Jesus Christ have always been concerned for the one. Jesus Christ is our greatest example. He was surrounded by multitudes and spoke to thousands, yet He always had concern for the one. 'For the Son of man is come to save that which was lost" [Matthew 18:11], He said. 'What man of you, having an hundred sheep, if he lose one of them, doth not leave the ninety and nine in the wilderness, and go after that which is lost, until he find it?' [Luke 15:4].

"This instruction applies to all who follow Him. We are commanded to seek out those who are lost. We are to be our brother's keeper. We cannot neglect this commission given by our Savior. *We must be concerned for the one*" ("Concern for the One," *Ensign,* May 2008. *Please note: emphasis to all quotations throughout the book has been added unless otherwise noted*).

Elder Wirthlin's explanation emphasizes two important implications that derive from the principle of *one by one*. First, the Savior knows, is concerned about, and loves each of us as a unique individual.

And second, each of us as a disciple of the Master has a responsibility to minister to others and recognize that what we do truly matters, even if what we do may seem small or inconsequential. As Elder Neal A. Maxwell observed, "That same God that placed that star in a precise orbit millennia before it appeared over Bethlehem in celebration of the birth of the Babe has given at least equal attention to placement of each of us in *precise human orbits* so that we may, if we will, illuminate the landscape of our individual lives, so that our light may not only lead others but warm them as well" (*That My Family Should Partake* [1974], 86).

THE LESSON IS ENRICHED

I first became aware of and gained experience with the principle of *one by one* long before my call to serve as a member of the Quorum of the Twelve Apostles. I recall with fondness the lessons I learned from my faithful mother. She was a model of ministering *one by one*. Aunts, uncles, and cousins selflessly served and were tremendous and tireless examples to me. The devoted priesthood and auxiliary leaders, advisers, and teachers of my youth consistently reinforced the importance of helping and blessing individuals *one by one*. And opportunities to serve as a priesthood leader throughout my life enriched greatly my understanding of ministering *one by one*.

The single greatest human exemplar of the principle of *one by one* with whom I am familiar is Susan Bednar, my wife. For many years, I have witnessed her individualized love and attention directed to me, to our children, to our growing family, to her parents and siblings, to the friends and associates of our children, to the sisters she serves as a visiting teacher, to the members of the wards we attend, to our neighbors, and to countless people around the world. Susan's prayers provide a rich tutorial in the principle of *one by one*.

Since my call to the Twelve, however, a consistent pattern of simple and profound experiences has enriched my understanding of this principle and enables me to bear solemn and sure witness that the Lord knows us *one by one*. He knows each of us. He knows our names. He knows our concerns. He knows our apprehensions. He knows our potential and possibilities.

The very sequence of events that ushered in this latter-day dispensation teaches us vital lessons. The appearance of the Eternal Father and His Beloved Son, Jesus Christ, to the boy Joseph Smith in 1820 is commonly referred to as the First Vision. The word *first* in this title is both important and accurate precisely because this holy event initiated the Restoration of the gospel in the dispensation of the fulness of times. This visitation affirmed the reality and existence of the Father and the Son, revealed much about Their true character, and is the ultimate source of correct knowledge about the existence and nature of God.

The Prophet Joseph Smith recounted his miraculous experience in the following words. "When the light rested upon me I saw two Personages, whose brightness and glory defy all description, standing above me in the air. One of them spake unto me, *calling me by name* and said, pointing to the other—*This is My Beloved Son. Hear Him!* (Joseph Smith—History 1:17).

Significantly, the first word spoken by God the Eternal Father to man in the first vision in this latter-day dispensation was *Joseph.* The Father and the Son knew Joseph Smith as a *one.*

Any call to serve the Savior in any capacity is an invitation to learn about the principle of *one by one,* because that was the pattern of His service. His work is focused first, foremost, and always upon serving people—not directing programs. Ministering and blessing are His work—not simply managing His Church as an organization. The scriptures are replete with examples of the Savior ministering to individuals. In fact, most recorded accounts of the Lord's mortal ministry are focused upon His teaching and blessing people *one by one.*

In a revelation given to Joseph Smith the Prophet, Oliver Cowdery, and David Whitmer in June of 1829, the Savior identified the spiritual reason for the work of ministering to individuals.

> Remember the worth of souls is great in the sight of God;
>
> And if it so be that you should labor all your days in crying repentance unto this people, and bring, save it be *one soul* unto me, how great shall be your joy with him in the kingdom of my Father.
>
> And now, if your joy will be great with *one soul* that you have brought unto me into the kingdom of my Father, how great will be your joy if you should bring *many souls* unto me! (Doctrine and Covenants 18:10, 15–16).

More recently, President Gordon B. Hinckley admonished, "We must look after the individual. Christ always spoke of individuals. He healed the sick, individually. He spoke in His parables of individuals. This Church is concerned with individuals, notwithstanding our numbers. Whether they be 6 or 10 or 12 or 50 million, we must never lose sight of the fact that the individual is the important thing" (*Teachings of Presidents of the Church: Gordon B. Hinckley* [2016], 298).

A call to serve as a special witness of the name of Christ in all of the world (see Doctrine and Covenants 107:23) and as a member of the Quorum of the Twelve requires a man to "learn of [Him], and listen to [His] words; [to] walk in the meekness of [His] Spirit" (Doctrine and Covenants 19:23), to follow His example, and to employ His pattern of ministering.

THE PATTERN CONTINUES

After my first experience as a member of the Twelve on that first weekend, I noticed over time the increasing frequency with which I had similar interactions with individuals and families on every assignment—and even when I was not on an assignment.

One day I was repairing the roof on our home. Because I had run out of nails and other materials necessary to finish my task, I went to a local store to purchase the required items. I was wearing my customary work clothes—casual pants and shoes, a well-worn T-shirt, and a baseball hat. Wanting to quickly return home and complete my project, I hurriedly entered the store and began looking for the things I needed.

A man approached me as I was selecting my supplies. He

observed, "Elder Bednar, the disguise is not working." We laughed, and then he inquired, "Do you mind if I ask you a question?"

I responded, "Well, that is why I am here."

He replied quizzically, "What do you mean?"

I said, "You are the reason I am here. I am doing repair work at my home, and I need a few things to finish the task on which I am working. But I am not in this store simply to buy roofing nails. I am here because God knew we were going to meet each other in this store and that you had something about which you wanted to ask. Please go ahead and share with me your question."

We talked in the aisle for about fifteen minutes, and I tried to help him find the answer to his question.

Was it merely a coincidence that I encountered this good man at the local store? Or was this episode divinely orchestrated by a loving Savior who knew and responded to the concerns of a faithful man—a *one?* I believe that in the work of the Lord there is no such thing as a coincidence. The worth of souls is great in the sight of God.

In a revelation given through the Prophet Joseph Smith in June of 1831, the Lord declared: "I will give unto you a pattern in all things, that ye may not be deceived; for Satan is abroad in the land, and he goeth forth deceiving the nations" (Doctrine and Covenants 52:14).

Please consider a specific phrase in this verse, *a pattern in all things.* Interestingly, the Lord gave us *a* and not *the* pattern in all things. I do not believe the Lord is suggesting with the language *a pattern in all things* that He has only one pattern to be used in every situation. Rather, the Lord's way includes a variety of patterns that can be employed to achieve different spiritual objectives.

Many spiritual patterns are evident in the life of the Savior and are described in the scriptures and in the teachings of living prophets and apostles. However, one of the patterns most characteristic of the Lord and His holy work is *one by one.* Through the episodes I have related and many, many more—episodes that are frequent, always individualized, and too numerous to count—the fundamental pattern of *one by one* that is inherent in the Lord's work has distilled upon my soul more completely and powerfully than ever before.

Acting under the direction of the First Presidency, the Twelve are "to build up the church, and regulate all the affairs of the same in all nations" (Doctrine and Covenants 107:33). This worldwide ministry and responsibility is accomplished by teaching and testifying in conferences, training priesthood and auxiliary leaders, participating in the Church's governing councils and committees, meeting with governmental, educational, and other officials, attending and assisting with temple dedications, and fulfilling a variety of other assignments. All of these activities are essential and important in the Savior's restored Church.

Each member of the Twelve also has a personal ministry focused upon and directed to *ones.* I have learned that my schedule of assignments around the world enables me not only to testify of the

Lord and assist in building up and regulating His Church, but also to travel to the places where He wants me to be to assist Him in blessing individuals and families according to His will and timing.

It is important to understand that the Savior does not send only General Authorities, general auxiliary leaders, stake presidents, bishops, Relief Society presidents, and other auxiliary leaders to minister single-handedly to the needs of every member in all units of His restored Church. Rather, He invites all Latter-day Saints—wherever we may live and in whatever capacity or calling we may serve—to fulfill important responsibilities and roles in the great work of the ministry.

This is not to say that every interaction we have with others should be considered to be a specific errand from the Lord. It might be easy for some to become overzealous and step beyond the boundaries of their own stewardships in presuming to receive inspiration for others. But as the Spirit directs, we all have opportunities to serve in the Lord's way.

This simple pattern of *one by one* influences everything I do, every day of my life and every place I go. For example, as I stand to speak in a meeting, I do not see a congregation of 100, 1,000, 2,000, or 20,000 people. Rather, with the Lord's help I strive to see 100, 1,000, 2,000, or 20,000 *ones*. I have learned there are no such things as large congregations; there are only large gatherings of *ones*. We do not speak to audiences; we speak to assembled *ones*.

Elder M. Russell Ballard taught: "Sadly, in today's world, a person's importance is often judged by the size of the audience before which he or she performs. That is how media and sports programs are rated, how corporate prominence is sometimes determined, and often how governmental rank is obtained. That may be why roles such as father, mother, and missionary seldom receive standing ovations. Fathers, mothers, and missionaries 'play' before very small audiences. Yet, in the eyes of the Lord, there may be only one size of audience that is of lasting importance—and that is just one, each one, you and me, and each one of the children of God. The irony of the Atonement is that it is infinite and eternal, yet it is applied individually, *one person at a time*" ("The Atonement and the Value of One Soul," *Ensign,* May 2004).

A SPIRITUAL PATTERN
REPEATED—AGAIN AND AGAIN

Many of my General Authority and general auxiliary associates have related their personal experiences in witnessing the Lord's pattern of ministering *one by one.*

Elder Merrill J. Bateman was serving as a member of the First Quorum of the Seventy and as the president of Brigham Young University at the time he shared the following story.

"The incident concerns a young woman who desired to attend BYU from the time she was very young but believed she would never have the opportunity because of difficult financial circumstances. Consequently, she did not apply during her senior year in high school even though her grades were excellent and she was worthy.

"As is customary, university advisement personnel hold meetings for newly selected freshmen each spring. On the day this meeting was held in her hometown, the young woman received in the mail a notice that she was a National Merit finalist. This meant her tuition would be paid by a national scholarship. Still, she did not have the financial means to cover the additional costs associated with moving from home and living in another state and city. However, the confluence of the notice and the meeting for new BYU freshmen rekindled a spark of hope, and she decided to attend even though she was not on the invitation list.

"I happened to be in the city that day on other business and was invited by our advisement people to speak to the new freshmen at the evening gathering. Following the main session, the freshmen were divided into small discussion groups and sent to other parts of the building. As I left the chapel, I stopped momentarily to visit with waiting parents. While conversing, I suddenly felt the presence of someone behind me. The feeling was followed by an impression that my help was needed. I turned, and there stood two women a few feet distant quietly conversing. They noticed my movement and looked up. I could tell they were waiting to see me. As I approached them, the mother introduced herself and indicated that her daughter would like to ask some questions. The young woman told me of her lifelong dream to attend Brigham Young University and how because of financial circumstances she had not applied. She then proceeded to tell me of the letter that had arrived that day notifying her of the National Merit Scholarship. She further stated that even though her tuition could be paid, her circumstances were such that it still appeared impossible to attend. She then asked if I knew of any way a door might be opened. As I listened, the thought came that her hope had been rekindled by the Holy Spirit and that I had been made aware of her presence by the same source. Additional thoughts came regarding university resources, including student jobs that are available. With the help of BYU admissions personnel, a way was found for the young woman to attend" ("One by One," *Brigham Young University Speeches, 1997–1998*, 1–2).

Was it merely a coincidence that Elder Bateman "happened to be in the city that day"? Or was this episode divinely orchestrated by a loving Lord who knew and responded to the yearnings of a young woman—a *one?* I believe that in the work of the Lord there is no such thing as a coincidence. The worth of souls is great in the sight of God.

Elder Ronald A. Rasband described in general conference a *one-by-one* experience he had with a missionary during his service as a mission president.

"During the final months of our mission . . . , we experienced an event that taught once again this profound principle that each of us is known and loved by God.

"Elder Neal A. Maxwell was coming to New York City for some Church business, and we were informed that he would also like to have a mission conference. We were so pleased to have this opportunity to hear from one of the Lord's chosen servants. I was asked to select one of our missionaries to provide the opening prayer for the meeting. I might have randomly picked one of the missionaries to pray, but felt to ponder and prayerfully select one whom the Lord would have me ask. In going through the missionary roster, a name boldly stood out to me: Elder Joseph Appiah of Accra, Ghana. He was the one I felt the Lord wanted to pray at the meeting.

"Prior to the mission conference, I was having a regularly scheduled interview with Elder Appiah and told him of the prompting that I had received for him to pray. With amazement and humility in his eyes, he began to weep deeply. Somewhat surprised by his reaction, I started to tell him that it was all right and he wouldn't have to pray, when he informed me he would love to offer the prayer, that his emotion was caused by the love he has for Elder Maxwell. He told me that this Apostle is very special to the Saints in Ghana and to his own family. Elder Maxwell had called his father to be the district president in Accra and had sealed his mother and father in the Salt Lake Temple.

"Now, I didn't know any of what I just related about this missionary or his family, but the Lord did and inspired a mission president on behalf of *one* missionary to provide a lifelong memory and testimony-building experience.

"At the meeting, Elder Appiah offered a wonderful prayer and made a humble contribution to a meeting where Elder Maxwell taught the missionaries of the attributes of Jesus Christ. All who were there will never forget the feelings of love they experienced for their Savior" ("One by One," *Ensign,* November 2000; emphasis in original).

Was it merely a coincidence that President Rasband selected Elder Appiah to offer the benediction in the missionary meeting with Elder Maxwell? Or was this episode divinely orchestrated by a loving Savior who knew and responded to the needs of a young missionary from Ghana—a *one?* I believe that in the work of the Lord there is no such thing as a coincidence. The worth of souls is great in the sight of God.

In his first address in general conference as a newly called General Authority Seventy, Elder Wm. Rolfe Kerr emphasized the individual and *one-by-one* nature of the Savior's ministry to the children in the multitude gathered at the temple in the land of Bountiful.

"When the Savior invited the multitude to behold their little ones, was He speaking in the collective sense of a group of little children? Or was He drawing their attention, and ours, to the individual nature and importance of each of those little *ones*— each of those little individuals? I believe that by His example the Savior was teaching us of the individual and tender care we should give to each one of our little children—indeed to each of our Heavenly Father's children. It may be the lovable toddler or the wayward teen, the grieving widow or the grateful woman for whom all is well. It may even be your own son or daughter or your own husband or wife. Each is an individual. Each has divine potential. And each must be spiritually nourished and temporally cared for with love, tenderness, and individual attention" ("'Behold Your Little Ones,'" *Ensign,* November 1996; emphasis in original).

Sister Linda K. Burton described in general conference the need for each of us to "first observe, then serve."

"For some, serving or ministering *one by one,* following the Savior's example, doesn't come easily. But with practice, each of us can become more like the Savior as we serve God's children. To help us better love one another, I would like to suggest four words to remember: 'First observe, then serve.'

"Almost 40 years ago my husband and I went to the temple for our Friday night date. We had been married only a short time, and I was nervous because this was only my second time as a newly-wed. A sister sitting next to me must have noticed. She leaned over and whispered reverently, 'Don't worry. I'll help you.' My fears were calmed, and I was able to enjoy the rest of the temple session. She first observed, then served. . . .

"A few weeks ago, I was hurried and frazzled, with too many to-dos on my list. I had hoped to go to the temple that day but felt I was just too busy. As soon as that thought of being too busy for temple service crossed my mind, it awakened me to what I most needed to do. I left my office to walk over to the Salt Lake Temple, wondering when I was going to recapture the time I was losing. Thankfully, the Lord is patient and merciful and taught me a beautiful lesson that day.

"As I sat down in the session room, a young sister leaned over and reverently whispered, 'I'm really nervous. This is only my second time in the temple. Could you please help me?' How could she ever have known that those words were exactly what I needed to hear? She didn't know, but Heavenly Father knew. He had observed my greatest need. I needed to serve. He prompted this humble young sister to serve me by inviting me to serve her. I assure you that I was the one who benefited most" ("First Observe, Then Serve," *Ensign,* November 2012).

Was it merely a coincidence that Sister Burton was in the right place at the right time to minister to a nervous young sister and learn a vital lesson? Or was this episode divinely orchestrated by a loving Savior who knew and responded simultaneously to the needs of two righteous women—two *ones?* I believe that in the work of the Lord there is no such thing as a coincidence. The worth of souls is great in the sight of God.

President Thomas S. Monson is one of the greatest examples of the Lord's pattern of ministering *one by one.* His ministry as a young bishop among the widows of his ward—more than eighty of them!—is legendary. His public sermons frequently feature life experiences emphasizing the importance of identifying and responding to the needs of individuals.

He learned a vital lesson about this principle early in his ministry: "As a young bishop, [President Monson] received a call one evening informing him that an older member of his ward had been taken to the veterans' hospital in Salt Lake City for treatment. Could he come to give the man a blessing? he was asked. Bishop Monson explained that he was just on his way to a stake meeting, but he would stop by the hospital as soon as the meeting was over. At that leadership meeting, he felt unsettled, ill at ease. A prompting came strongly: leave the meeting at once, and go directly to the hospital. But surely it would be discourteous to walk out while the stake president was speaking, wouldn't it? He waited until the end of the stake president's address and then made his way to the door even before the closing prayer. At the hospital he found himself running down the corridor. There seemed to be a flurry of activity outside the man's room, and a nurse stopped the new arrival. 'Are you Bishop Monson?' she asked. 'Yes,' was his anxious reply. 'I'm sorry,' the nurse replied. 'The patient was calling your name just before he passed away.'

"As the young bishop walked out of the hospital that night, he vowed he would never again fail to act on an impression from the Lord. No man could have been more true to that vow. Indeed, his life has been one miracle after another in response to his faithful adherence to promptings of the Spirit."

The lesson President Monson learned as a bishop has served him well throughout his apostolic ministry. One further example will illustrate:

"As a member of the Quorum of the Twelve Apostles . . . he had originally been assigned to visit another stake [on a particular] weekend, but there was a need to change the assignment. Elder Monson knew of no special significance to the place when President Ezra Taft Benson (1899–1994), then President of the Quorum of the Twelve, said, 'Brother Monson, I feel impressed to have you visit the Shreveport Louisiana Stake.'

"Arriving in Shreveport, Elder Monson learned of 10-year-old Christal Methvin, suffering from terminal cancer, who had a desire to receive a blessing from one General Authority in particular—him. He studied the schedule of conference meetings and found there was no time for the 80-mile (130-km) trip to Christal's home. He asked the stake president to have Christal remembered in the public prayers during the stake conference. The Methvin family understood the travel problem but prayed, nevertheless, that their daughter's desire might be realized. Elder Monson was preparing to speak in the Saturday evening leadership meeting when, as he recalls, 'I heard a voice speak to my spirit. The message was brief, the words familiar: "Suffer the little children to come unto me, and forbid them not: for of such is the kingdom of God" (Mark 10:14).' With the help of the stake president, a visit to the Methvin home was quickly arranged for the following morning. It was a solemn and sacred experience for those involved. Only four days after receiving the desired blessing, Christal returned home to her Heavenly Father.

"Frequently, events such as this one created spiritual ripple effects in the lives of others. Speaking in general conference in October 1975, Elder Monson shared Christal's story. Seeing a little blonde girl of about Christal's age in the balcony of the Tabernacle, he felt moved to address his remarks to her. After relating the story of Christal's heartfelt desire that Heavenly Father lovingly honored, Elder Monson said in conclusion, 'To you, my little friend in the upper balcony, and to believers everywhere, I bear witness that Jesus of Nazareth does love little children, that He listens to your prayers and responds to them.'

"When Elder Monson returned to his office after that session of conference, he found the young blonde girl from the balcony waiting for him with her grandmother. The little girl had been trying to decide whether to be baptized; someone close to her had advised her to wait until she was 18. She had asked her grandmother to take her to conference, with faith that Jesus would help her find an answer. Taking Elder Monson's hand, she said, 'You helped Him answer my prayer. Thank you.' She was baptized soon afterward" (Jeffrey R. Holland, "President Thomas S. Monson: In the Footsteps of the Master," *Liahona,* June 2008).

"HELP THOU MINE UNBELIEF"

I suspect some individuals may be thinking to themselves at this point—surely the President of the Church, General Authorities, the General Relief Society President, and people called to serve in prominent stake and ward callings have *one-by-one* experiences like those described in this chapter. But I do not. I believe the Lord does indeed minister *one by one*. But not to me or through me.

I am acquainted with Church members who accept as true the doctrine and principles contained in the scriptures and proclaimed in general conference. And yet they have a hard time believing that those gospel truths apply specifically in their lives and to their circumstances. They seem to have faith in the Savior, but they do not believe that His promised blessings are available to them or can operate in their lives. I also encounter brothers and sisters who fulfill their Church callings dutifully, but for whom the restored gospel has not yet become a living and transforming reality in their lives. We come to know the Lord as we not only believe in Him but also believe Him and His assurances.

In the New Testament, a father asked the Savior to heal his child. Jesus answered, "If thou canst believe, all things are possible to him that believeth.

"And straightway the father of the child cried out, and said with tears, Lord, I believe; help thou mine unbelief" (Mark 9:23–24).

I have reflected many times on this father's request, "help thou mine unbelief." I wonder if the intent of the man's pleading was not primarily to help him believe in Jesus as our Redeemer and in His healing power. He already may have acknowledged Christ as the Son of God. But perhaps he needed help to believe the Master's healing power indeed could be so individual and so personalized as to bless his own beloved child as a *one*. He may have believed in Christ generally but not believed that he specifically and personally could be the recipient of the Savior's love and *one-by-one* ministering.

We often testify of what we know to be true, but perhaps the more relevant question for each of us is whether we believe what we know.

Sacred ordinances performed by proper priesthood authority are essential to believing the Savior, coming to know Him, and, ultimately, believing what we know.

"And [the Melchizedek] priesthood administereth the gospel and holdeth the key of the mysteries of the kingdom, even *the key of the knowledge of God.*

"Therefore, in the ordinances thereof, the power of godliness is manifest" (Doctrine and Covenants 84:19–20).

We believe and come to know the Lord as the key of the knowledge of God administered through the Melchizedek Priesthood unlocks the door and makes it possible for each of us to receive the power of godliness in our lives. We believe and come to know the Savior as we follow Him by receiving and faithfully honoring holy ordinances and thus increasingly have His image in our countenances. We believe and come to know Christ as we experience personally the transforming, healing, strengthening, and sanctifying power of His Atonement. We believe and come to know the Master as "the power of his word [takes root] . . . in us" (Alma 26:13) and is written in our minds and hearts (see Hebrews 8:10), and we "give away all [our] sins to know [Him]" (Alma 22:18).

Believing Him is trusting that His bounteous blessings are available and applicable to us *one by one* in our individual lives and families. Believing Him is acknowledging that He knows our names and will provide the individual guidance and help we need. Believing Him is relying upon His inspiration and guidance as we strive to minister to and bless those whom we serve *one by one*. Believing Him with our whole soul (see Omni 1:26) comes as we press forward along the covenant pathway, surrender our will to His, and submit to His priorities and timing for us. Believing Him—accepting as true His power and promises—invites perspective and peace into our lives.

President Henry B. Eyring described in general conference a pattern that helps him to see and remember the bounteous blessings bestowed by the Lord upon him and his family.

"I would ponder this question: 'Have I seen the hand of God reaching out to touch us or our children or our family today?' As

I kept at it, something began to happen. As I would cast my mind over the day, I would see evidence of what God had done for one of us that I had not recognized in the busy moments of the day. As that happened, and it happened often, I realized that trying to remember had allowed God to show me what He had done.

"More than gratitude began to grow in my heart. Testimony grew. I became ever more certain that our Heavenly Father hears and answers prayers. I felt more gratitude for the softening and refining that come because of the Atonement of the Savior Jesus Christ. And I grew more confident that the Holy Ghost can bring all things to our remembrance—even things we did not notice or pay attention to when they happened. . . .

"My point is to urge you to find ways to recognize and remember God's kindness. It will build our testimonies. . . . You . . . will be blessed as you remember what the Lord has done. . . .

"Tonight, and tomorrow night, you might pray and ponder, asking the questions: Did God send a message that was just for me? Did I see His hand in my life or the lives of my children? I will do that. And then I will find a way to preserve that memory for the day that I, and those that I love, will need to remember how much God loves us and how much we need Him. I testify that He loves us and blesses us, more than most of us have yet recognized" ("O Remember, Remember," *Ensign,* November 2007).

SUMMARY

One of the important lessons I have learned during my years of service as a member of the Quorum of the Twelve Apostles in The Church of Jesus Christ of Latter-day Saints is that the Lord knows each of us individually and loves each of us infinitely. He knows us *one by one* and name by name.

As I have traveled throughout the world on the Lord's errand, I have felt an increasing dissatisfaction with human language to adequately describe the breadth, the depth, the comprehensiveness, and the eternal importance of the things I have been blessed to observe, to learn, and to feel. I do not know and cannot comprehend how God divinely and simultaneously orchestrates so many spiritually vital encounters in the lives of people all over the world. But I know that He does.

"[His] thoughts are not [our] thoughts, neither are [our] ways [His] ways, saith the Lord.

"For as the heavens are higher than the earth, so are [His] ways higher than [our] ways, and [His] thoughts than [our] thoughts" (Isaiah 55:8–9).

I am a witness to an overwhelming abundance of "the evidence of things not seen" (Hebrews 11:1). And I joyfully declare God lives, He knows each of us, and He loves us.

Elder Neal A. Maxwell frequently taught that, as we invite Him, the Lord is involved in the details of our lives.

"So it is, amid the vastness of His creations, God's personal shaping influence is felt in the details of our lives—not only in the details of the galaxies and molecules but, much more importantly, in the details of our own lives. Somehow God is providing these individual tutorials for us while at the same time He is overseeing cosmic funerals and births, for as one earth passes away so another is born (see Moses 1:38). It is marvelous that He would attend to us so personally in the midst of those cosmic duties. . . .

"Be assured that God is in the details and in the subtleties of the defining and preparatory moments of discipleship. He will reassure you. He will remind you. Sometimes, if you're like me, He will brace or reprove you in a highly personal process not understood or appreciated by those outside the context" ("Becoming a Disciple," *Ensign,* June 1996).

I began this chapter by describing an experience I had during my first weekend assignment as a member of the Twelve and the lesson that was reinforced for me about the Lord's pattern of ministering *one by one.* I conclude this chapter by recounting an experience I had recently while traveling home from another weekend assignment.

My companion for this weekend was a newly called General Authority Seventy. Customarily, the new Brethren have a series of training activities with members of the Twelve. And we had spent the weekend together listening, observing, teaching, testifying, training, and answering questions with members and priesthood and auxiliary leaders. We enjoyed a marvelous weekend serving together.

As we were scheduled to sit in adjacent seats on our flight home, we both looked forward to reviewing, debriefing, and discussing the events of the weekend. The trip provided a perfect opportunity for us to talk about the things we had observed and learned and to identify ways we could improve.

As I boarded the plane, the gate attendant informed me that my seat assignment had been changed. A mechanical problem with the aircraft on which we originally were scheduled to fly had necessitated a change of equipment, and the new plane on which we would be flying had a different seat configuration. Thus, my seat was altered. I also learned I would not be seated next to my General Authority Seventy companion. As I walked down the boarding ramp, I determined I would simply ask a person on the flight to switch seats with me so my companion and I could sit together and productively use our time.

As I settled into my seat on the plane, I began looking for the person whom I might invite to switch seats. However, I felt constrained and did not act. I simply had a sense that I should wait and see what would happen.

A few minutes later a woman made her way to her seat next to me and sat down. Without saying a word, she stowed her carry-on bag and other belongings and quickly put on her headphones. I initially thought the woman intended to hunker down on this late-night flight and immerse herself in her digital device. And yet, I still felt I should not attempt to change seats. As we taxied to the runway for takeoff, I retrieved a folder from my briefcase and began reviewing materials and making notes for an upcoming presentation I was scheduled to make.

Approximately thirty minutes later, the woman seated next to me took off her headphones and said, "Elder Bednar, I have been reluctant to disturb you. I know people are always asking you questions or seeking your advice, and I did not want to bother you. But do you mind if I ask you a question?"

We spent nearly two hours talking about a vexing problem through which this sister was attempting to work. She finally looked at me and said, "Thank you for talking with me, but I have taken too much of your time. I need to let you get back to your work."

I then suggested to her that in the work of the Lord there is no such thing as a coincidence, and we were seated next to each other on that flight for a reason. I testified that God knew her name and was aware of her personal circumstances and concerns. "In fact," I said to her, "the very purpose for my trip across the country this weekend may have been to be on this plane at this time so we could have this conversation. I believe that is why our seats were changed." As our plane landed in Salt Lake City, I again bore my witness to this good sister that the Lord would guide, direct, and inspire her.

Was it merely a coincidence that this woman and I ended up seated next to each other on that flight? Or was this episode divinely orchestrated by a loving Redeemer who knew and responded to the apprehensions and fears of a faithful woman—a *one?* I believe that in the work of the Lord there is no such thing as a coincidence. The worth of souls is great in the sight of God.

Elder M. Russell Ballard noted: "I believe that if we could truly understand the Atonement of the Lord Jesus Christ, we would realize how precious is *one* son or daughter of God. I believe our Heavenly Father's everlasting purpose for His children is generally achieved by the small and simple things we do for one another. At the heart of the English word *atonement* is the word *one.* If all mankind understood this, there would never be anyone with whom we would not be concerned, regardless of age, race, gender, religion, or social or economic standing. We would strive to emulate the Savior and would never be unkind, indifferent, disrespectful, or insensitive to others" (The Atonement and the Value of One Soul," *Ensign,* May 2004; emphasis in original).

The fundamental pattern of *one by one* that is inherent in the Lord's work is His, it is real, and it blesses each of us.

Questions to Consider

1. What can and should I do in my life to continue learning about the spiritual pattern of ministering *one by one?*

2. How does increasing my understanding of the spiritual pattern

of ministering *one by one* affect my heart, my motives, and my behavior?

3. What can and should I do to recognize and believe more fully in the spiritual pattern of *one by one* in my own life and in the lives of others?

My Own Questions to Consider

1. _____

_____

2. _____

_____

3. _____

_____

Scriptures Related to What I Am Learning

_____

_____

_____

CHAPTER 2

ONE BY ONE AND THE EXAMPLE OF JESUS CHRIST

As mentioned earlier, the Lord has identified in the scriptures the essential rationale for His spiritual pattern of ministering *one by one.*

Remember the worth of souls is great in the sight of God;

For, behold, the Lord your Redeemer suffered death in the flesh; wherefore he suffered the pain of all men, that all men might repent and come unto him.

And he hath risen again from the dead, that he might bring *all men* unto him, on conditions of repentance.

> And how great is his joy in *the soul* that repenteth!
>
> Wherefore, you are called to cry repentance unto this people.
>
> And if it so be that you should labor all your days in crying repentance unto this people, and bring, save it be *one soul* unto me, how great shall be your joy with him in the kingdom of my Father!
>
> And now, if your joy will be great with *one soul* that you have brought unto me into the kingdom of my Father, how great will be your joy if you should bring *many souls* unto me! (Doctrine and Covenants 18:10–16)

Please note the singularity of the Savior's emphasis upon *the soul* and *one soul,* even though His redeeming mission is to bring "all men unto him, on conditions of repentance." And the Redeemer's consistent focus upon the worth of an individual inspires even greater awe and wonderment as we consider the incomprehensible breadth, depth, and scope of His Father's eternal work.

> And worlds without number have I created; and I also created them for mine own purpose; and by the Son I created them, which is mine Only Begotten.
>
> And as one earth shall pass away, and the heavens

thereof even so shall another come; and there is no end to my works, neither to my words.

For behold, this is my work and my glory—to bring to pass the immortality and eternal life of man. (Moses 1:33, 38–39)

In the expanse of eternity and among all of God's creations, the Father and the Son are concerned about individuals—about each and every individual *one*.

President Dieter F. Uchtdorf observed, "And while we may look at the vast expanse of the universe and say, 'What is man in comparison to the glory of creation?' God Himself said we are the reason He created the universe! His work and glory—the purpose for this magnificent universe—is to save and exalt mankind. In other words, the vast expanse of eternity, the glories and mysteries of infinite space and time are all built for the benefit of ordinary mortals like you and me. Our Heavenly Father created the universe that we might reach our potential as His sons and daughters.

"This is a paradox of man: compared to God, man is nothing; yet we are everything to God. While against the backdrop of infinite creation we may appear to be nothing, we have a spark of eternal fire burning within our breast. We have the incomprehensible promise of exaltation—worlds without end—within our grasp. And it is God's great desire to help us reach it" ("You Matter to Him," *Ensign,* November 2011).

EXAMPLES OF ONE BY ONE
IN THE NEW TESTAMENT

Jesus Christ was sinless and divinely selfless. His true character of turning outward to bless and serve others is revealed repeatedly in the holy scriptures and is evidenced in His pattern of ministering *one by one.*

President Howard W. Hunter said: "In the press of a multitude, he sensed the singular touch of a woman who sought relief for an ailment from which she had suffered for some twelve years. (See Luke 8:43–48.) On another occasion, he saw beyond the narrowly focused prejudice of a condemning crowd and the sin of her who stood accused. Perhaps sensing her willingness to repent, Christ chose to see the worth of the individual and sent her forth to sin no more. (See John 8:1–11.) On another occasion, 'he took their little children, *one by one,* and blessed them, and prayed unto the Father for them.' (3 Ne. 17:21; italics added.)

"As the trials of Gethsemane and Calvary fast approached, with much weighing heavily upon his mind, the Savior took time to notice the widow casting in her mite. (See Mark 12:41–44). Similarly, his gaze took in the small-statured Zacchaeus who, unable to see because of the size of those congregating around the Savior, had climbed a sycamore tree for a view of the Son of God. (See Luke 19:1–5.) While hanging in agony upon the cross, he overlooked his own suffering and reached out in caring concern to the weeping woman who had given him life. (See John 19:25–27)" (Howard W. Hunter, "The Church Is for All People," *Ensign,* June 1989).

As you read the following parables and episodes from the New Testament, I invite you to prayerfully identify and ponder the Savior's pattern of *one by one.* As you study with real intent and a sincere heart (see Moroni 10:3–5), the Holy Ghost will help you identify in these scriptures truths and insights you previously may not have recognized. Your understanding of the character of the Savior also will be enlarged and enriched.

These examples are intended to be representative but not exhaustive. And the episodes are not presented in any particular order or sequence.

I offer only one repeated sentence of commentary at the end of each episode. I employ this approach so the unfiltered scriptural text, the influence of the Spirit, and the powerful cumulative effect of these accounts can speak directly to your mind and heart (see Doctrine and Covenants 8:2–3).

JESUS REVEALS THINGS TO NATHANAEL (JOHN 1:45-51)

Philip findeth Nathanael, and saith unto him, We have found him, of whom Moses in the law, and the prophets, did write, Jesus of Nazareth, the son of Joseph.

And Nathanael said unto him, Can there any

good thing come out of Nazareth? Philip saith unto him, Come and see.

Jesus saw Nathanael coming to him, and saith of him, Behold an Israelite indeed, in whom is no guile!

Nathanael saith unto him, Whence knowest thou me? Jesus answered and said unto him, Before that Philip called thee, when thou wast under the fig tree, I saw thee.

Nathanael answered and saith unto him, Rabbi, thou art the Son of God; thou art the King of Israel.

Jesus answered and said unto him, Because I said unto thee, I saw thee under the fig tree, believest thou? thou shalt see greater things than these.

And he saith unto him, Verily, verily, I say unto you, Hereafter ye shall see heaven open, and the angels of God ascending and descending upon the Son of man.

The story of Jesus revealing things to Nathanael is a story about a *one*—because the worth of souls is great in the sight of God.

JESUS TEACHES NICODEMUS ALONE AT NIGHT (JOHN 3:1-13)

There was a man of the Pharisees, named Nicodemus, a ruler of the Jews:

The same came to Jesus by night, and said unto

him, Rabbi, we know that thou art a teacher come from God: for no man can do these miracles that thou doest, except God be with him.

Jesus answered and said unto him, Verily, verily, I say unto thee, Except a man be born again, he cannot see the kingdom of God.

Nicodemus saith unto him, How can a man be born when he is old? can he enter the second time into his mother's womb, and be born?

Jesus answered, Verily, verily, I say unto thee, Except a man be born of water and of the Spirit, he cannot enter into the kingdom of God.

That which is born of the flesh is flesh; and that which is born of the Spirit is spirit.

Marvel not that I said unto thee, Ye must be born again.

The wind bloweth where it listeth, and thou hearest the sound thereof, but canst not tell whence it cometh, and whither it goeth: so is every one that is born of the Spirit.

Nicodemus answered and said unto him, How can these things be?

Jesus answered and said unto him, Art thou a master of Israel, and knowest not these things?

Verily, verily, I say unto thee, We speak that we do

know, and testify that we have seen; and ye receive not our witness.

If I have told you earthly things, and ye believe not, how shall ye believe, if I tell you of heavenly things?

And no man hath ascended up to heaven, but he that came down from heaven, even the Son of man which is in heaven.

The story of Jesus teaching Nicodemus alone at night is a story about a *one*—because the worth of souls is great in the sight of God.

JESUS INDIVIDUALLY HEALS MANY WITH DIVERSE AFFLICTIONS (MATTHEW 4:23-24)

And Jesus went about all Galilee, teaching in their synagogues, and preaching the gospel of the kingdom, and healing all manner of sickness and all manner of disease among the people.

And his fame went throughout all Syria: and they brought unto him all sick people that were taken with divers diseases and torments, and those which were possessed with devils, and those which were lunatic, and those that had the palsy; and he healed them.

The story of Jesus individually healing people with diverse afflictions is a story about many *ones*—because the worth of souls is great in the sight of God.

JESUS HEALS EVERY ONE OF THE SICK
BROUGHT TO HIM (LUKE 4:40)

Now when the sun was setting, all they that had any sick with divers diseases brought them unto him; and he laid his hands on every one of them, and healed them.

The story of Jesus healing every sick person brought to him is a story about many *ones*—because the worth of souls is great in the sight of God.

JESUS TEACHES THE WOMAN AT THE WELL (JOHN 4:5-26)

Then cometh he to a city of Samaria, which is called Sychar, near to the parcel of ground that Jacob gave to his son Joseph.

Now Jacob's well was there. Jesus therefore, being wearied with his journey, sat thus on the well: and it was about the sixth hour.

There cometh a woman of Samaria to draw water: Jesus saith unto her, Give me to drink.

(For his disciples were gone away unto the city to buy meat.)

Then saith the woman of Samaria unto him, How is it that thou, being a Jew, askest drink of me, which am a woman of Samaria? for the Jews have no dealings with the Samaritans.

Jesus answered and said unto her, If thou knewest the gift of God, and who it is that saith to thee, Give me to drink; thou wouldest have asked of him, and he would have given thee living water.

The woman saith unto him, Sir, thou hast nothing to draw with, and the well is deep: from whence then hast thou that living water?

Art thou greater than our father Jacob, which gave us the well, and drank thereof himself, and his children, and his cattle?

Jesus answered and said unto her, Whosoever drinketh of this water shall thirst again:

But whosoever drinketh of the water that I shall give him shall never thirst; but the water that I shall give him shall be in him a well of water springing up into everlasting life.

The woman saith unto him, Sir, give me this water, that I thirst not, neither come hither to draw.

Jesus saith unto her, Go, call thy husband, and come hither.

The woman answered and said, I have no husband. Jesus said unto her, Thou hast well said, I have no husband:

For thou hast had five husbands; and he whom thou now hast is not thy husband: in that saidst thou truly.

The woman saith unto him, Sir, I perceive that thou art a prophet.

Our fathers worshipped in this mountain; and ye say, that in Jerusalem is the place where men ought to worship.

Jesus saith unto her, Woman, believe me, the hour cometh, when ye shall neither in this mountain, nor yet at Jerusalem, worship the Father.

Ye worship ye know not what: we know what we worship: for salvation is of the Jews.

But the hour cometh, and now is, when the true worshippers shall worship the Father in spirit and in truth: for the Father seeketh such to worship him.

God is a Spirit: and they that worship him must worship him in spirit and in truth.

The woman saith unto him, I know that Messias cometh, which is called Christ: when he is come, he will tell us all things.

Jesus saith unto her, I that speak unto thee am he.

The story of Jesus speaking to the woman at the well is a story about a *one*—because the worth of souls is great in the sight of God.

JESUS TEACHES THE WOMAN TAKEN IN ADULTERY
WHEN THEY ARE ALONE (JOHN 8:2-11)

And early in the morning he came again into the temple, and all the people came unto him; and he sat down, and taught them.

And the scribes and Pharisees brought unto him a woman taken in adultery; and when they had set her in the midst,

They say unto him, Master, this woman was taken in adultery, in the very act.

Now Moses in the law commanded us, that such should be stoned: but what sayest thou?

This they said, tempting him, that they might have to accuse him. But Jesus stooped down, and with his finger wrote on the ground, as though he heard them not.

So when they continued asking him, he lifted up himself, and said unto them, He that is without sin among you, let him first cast a stone at her.

And again he stooped down, and wrote on the ground.

And they which heard it, being convicted by their own conscience, went out one by one, beginning at the eldest, even unto the last: and Jesus was left alone, and the woman standing in the midst.

When Jesus had lifted up himself, and saw none but the woman, he said unto her, Woman, where are those thine accusers? hath no man condemned thee?

She said, No man, Lord. And Jesus said unto her, Neither do I condemn thee: go, and sin no more.

The story of Jesus teaching the woman taken in adultery is a story about a *one*—because the worth of souls is great in the sight of God.

THE WOMAN WHO TOUCHES THE SAVIOR'S GARMENT IS HEALED (LUKE 8:43–48)

And a woman having an issue of blood twelve years, which had spent all her living upon physicians, neither could be healed of any,

Came behind him, and touched the border of his garment: and immediately her issue of blood stanched.

And Jesus said, Who touched me? When all denied, Peter and they that were with him said, Master, the multitude throng thee and press thee, and sayest thou, Who touched me?

And Jesus said, Somebody hath touched me: for I perceive that virtue is gone out of me.

And when the woman saw that she was not hid, she came trembling, and falling down before him,

> she declared unto him before all the people for what cause she had touched him, and how she was healed immediately.
>
> And he said unto her, Daughter, be of good comfort: thy faith hath made thee whole; go in peace.

The story of the woman who touches the Savior's garment and is healed is a story about a *one*—because the worth of souls is great in the sight of God.

JESUS RAISES JAIRUS'S DAUGHTER FROM THE DEAD (LUKE 8:49–56)

> While he yet spake, there cometh one from the ruler of the synagogue's house, saying to him, Thy daughter is dead; trouble not the Master.
>
> But when Jesus heard it, he answered him, saying, Fear not: believe only, and she shall be made whole.
>
> And when he came into the house, he suffered no man to go in, save Peter, and James, and John, and the father and the mother of the maiden.
>
> And all wept, and bewailed her: but he said, Weep not; she is not dead, but sleepeth.
>
> And they laughed him to scorn, knowing that she was dead.

And he put them all out, and took her by the hand, and called, saying, Maid, arise.

And her spirit came again, and she arose straightway: and he commanded to give her meat.

And her parents were astonished: but he charged them that they should tell no man what was done.

The story of Jesus raising Jairus's daughter from the dead is a story about a *one*—because the worth of souls is great in the sight of God.

THE PARABLE OF THE GOOD SAMARITAN (LUKE 10:25–37)

And, behold, a certain lawyer stood up, and tempted him, saying, Master, what shall I do to inherit eternal life?

He said unto him, What is written in the law? how readest thou?

And he answering said, Thou shalt love the Lord thy God with all thy heart, and with all thy soul, and with all thy strength, and with all thy mind; and thy neighbour as thyself.

And he said unto him, Thou hast answered right: this do, and thou shalt live.

But he, willing to justify himself, said unto Jesus, And who is my neighbour?

And Jesus answering said, A certain man went down from Jerusalem to Jericho, and fell among thieves, which stripped him of his raiment, and wounded him, and departed, leaving him half dead.

And by chance there came down a certain priest that way: and when he saw him, he passed by on the other side.

And likewise a Levite, when he was at the place, came and looked on him, and passed by on the other side.

But a certain Samaritan, as he journeyed, came where he was: and when he saw him, he had compassion on him,

And went to him, and bound up his wounds, pouring in oil and wine, and set him on his own beast, and brought him to an inn, and took care of him.

And on the morrow when he departed, he took out two pence, and gave them to the host, and said unto him, Take care of him; and whatsoever thou spendest more, when I come again, I will repay thee.

Which now of these three, thinkest thou, was neighbour unto him that fell among the thieves?

And he said, He that shewed mercy on him. Then said Jesus unto him, Go, and do thou likewise.

The parable of the good Samaritan is a parable about a *one*—because the worth of souls is great in the sight of God.

JESUS WEEPS WITH MARY (JOHN 11:28-35)

And when she had so said, she went her way, and called Mary her sister secretly, saying, The Master is come, and calleth for thee.

As soon as she heard that, she arose quickly, and came unto him.

Now Jesus was not yet come into the town, but was in that place where Martha met him.

The Jews then which were with her in the house, and comforted her, when they saw Mary, that she rose up hastily and went out, followed her, saying, She goeth unto the grave to weep there.

Then when Mary was come where Jesus was, and saw him, she fell down at his feet, saying unto him, Lord, if thou hadst been here, my brother had not died.

When Jesus therefore saw her weeping, and the Jews also weeping which came with her, he groaned in the spirit, and was troubled,

And said, Where have ye laid him? They said unto him, Lord, come and see.

Jesus wept.

The story of Jesus weeping with Mary is a story about a *one*—because the worth of souls is great in the sight of God.

JESUS NOTICES THE WIDOW CASTING IN HER MITE (MARK 12:41-44)

And Jesus sat over against the treasury, and beheld how the people cast money into the treasury: and many that were rich cast in much.

And there came a certain poor widow, and she threw in two mites, which make a farthing.

And he called unto him his disciples, and saith unto them, Verily I say unto you, That this poor widow hath cast more in, than all they which have cast into the treasury:

For all they did cast in of their abundance; but she of her want did cast in all that she had, even all her living.

The story of Jesus noticing the widow casting in her mite is a story about a *one*—because the worth of souls is great in the sight of God.

JESUS HEALS A WOMAN ON THE SABBATH (LUKE 13:10-17)

And he was teaching in one of the synagogues on the sabbath.

And, behold, there was a woman which had a

spirit of infirmity eighteen years, and was bowed together, and could in no wise lift up herself.

And when Jesus saw her, he called her to him, and said unto her, Woman, thou art loosed from thine infirmity.

And he laid his hands on her: and immediately she was made straight, and glorified God.

And the ruler of the synagogue answered with indignation, because that Jesus had healed on the sabbath day, and said unto the people, There are six days in which men ought to work: in them therefore come and be healed, and not on the sabbath day.

The Lord then answered him, and said, Thou hypocrite, doth not each one of you on the sabbath loose his ox or his ass from the stall, and lead him away to watering?

And ought not this woman, being a daughter of Abraham, whom Satan hath bound, lo, these eighteen years, be loosed from this bond on the sabbath day?

And when he had said these things, all his adversaries were ashamed: and all the people rejoiced for all the glorious things that were done by him.

The story of Jesus healing the woman on the Sabbath is a story about a *one*—because the worth of souls is great in the sight of God.

THE PARABLE OF THE LOST SHEEP (LUKE 15:4-7)

What man of you, having an hundred sheep, if he lose one of them, doth not leave the ninety and nine in the wilderness, and go after that which is lost, until he find it?

And when he hath found it, he layeth it on his shoulders, rejoicing.

And when he cometh home, he calleth together his friends and neighbours, saying unto them, Rejoice with me; for I have found my sheep which was lost.

I say unto you, that likewise joy shall be in heaven over one sinner that repenteth, more than over ninety and nine just persons, which need no repentance.

The parable of the lost sheep is a parable about a *one*—because the worth of souls is great in the sight of God.

THE PARABLE OF THE PIECE OF SILVER (LUKE 15:8-10)

Either what woman having ten pieces of silver, if she lose one piece, doth not light a candle, and sweep the house, and seek diligently till she find it?

And when she hath found it, she calleth her

friends and her neighbours together, saying, Rejoice with me; for I have found the piece which I had lost.

Likewise, I say unto you, there is joy in the presence of the angels of God over one sinner that repenteth.

The parable of the piece of silver is a parable about a *one*—because the worth of souls is great in the sight of God.

THE PARABLE OF THE PRODIGAL SON (LUKE 15:11–24)

A certain man had two sons:

And the younger of them said to his father, Father, give me the portion of goods that falleth to me. And he divided unto them his living.

And not many days after the younger son gathered all together, and took his journey into a far country, and there wasted his substance with riotous living.

And when he had spent all, there arose a mighty famine in that land; and he began to be in want.

And he went and joined himself to a citizen of that country; and he sent him into his fields to feed swine.

And he would fain have filled his belly with the husks that the swine did eat: and no man gave unto him.

And when he came to himself, he said, How many

hired servants of my father's have bread enough and to spare, and I perish with hunger!

I will arise and go to my father, and will say unto him, Father, I have sinned against heaven, and before thee,

And am no more worthy to be called thy son: make me as one of thy hired servants.

And he arose, and came to his father. But when he was yet a great way off, his father saw him, and had compassion, and ran, and fell on his neck, and kissed him.

And the son said unto him, Father, I have sinned against heaven, and in thy sight, and am no more worthy to be called thy son.

But the father said to his servants, Bring forth the best robe, and put it on him; and put a ring on his hand, and shoes on his feet:

And bring hither the fatted calf, and kill it; and let us eat, and be merry:

For this my son was dead, and is alive again; he was lost, and is found. And they began to be merry.

The parable of the prodigal son is a parable about a *one*— because the worth of souls is great in the sight of God.

JESUS ACKNOWLEDGES ZACCHAEUS (LUKE 19:1-9)

And Jesus entered and passed through Jericho.

And, behold, there was a man named Zacchaeus, which was the chief among the publicans, and he was rich.

And he sought to see Jesus who he was; and could not for the press, because he was little of stature.

And he ran before, and climbed up into a sycomore tree to see him: for he was to pass that way.

And when Jesus came to the place, he looked up, and saw him, and said unto him, Zacchaeus, make haste, and come down; for to day I must abide at thy house.

And he made haste, and came down, and received him joyfully.

And when they saw it, they all murmured, saying, That he was gone to be guest with a man that is a sinner.

And Zacchaeus stood, and said unto the Lord; Behold, Lord, the half of my goods I give to the poor; and if I have taken any thing from any man by false accusation, I restore him fourfold.

And Jesus said unto him, This day is salvation

come to this house, forsomuch as he also is a son of
Abraham.

The story of Jesus acknowledging Zacchaeus is a story about
a *one*—because the worth of souls is great in the sight of God.

JESUS BLESSES LITTLE CHILDREN (MATTHEW 19:13-15)

Then were there brought unto him little children,
that he should put his hands on them, and pray: and
the disciples rebuked them.

But Jesus said, Suffer little children, and forbid
them not, to come unto me: for of such is the kingdom of heaven.

And he laid his hands on them, and departed
thence.

The story of Jesus blessing the children is a story about many
ones—because the worth of souls is great in the sight of God.

JESUS TEACHES A RICH YOUNG RULER (MATTHEW 19:16-26)

And, behold, one came and said unto him, Good
Master, what good thing shall I do, that I may have
eternal life?

And he said unto him, Why callest thou me good?
there is none good but one, that is, God: but if thou
wilt enter into life, keep the commandments.

He saith unto him, Which? Jesus said, Thou shalt do no murder, Thou shalt not commit adultery, Thou shalt not steal, Thou shalt not bear false witness,

Honour thy father and thy mother: and, Thou shalt love thy neighbour as thyself.

The young man saith unto him, All these things have I kept from my youth up: what lack I yet?

Jesus said unto him, If thou wilt be perfect, go and sell that thou hast, and give to the poor, and thou shalt have treasure in heaven: and come and follow me.

But when the young man heard that saying, he went away sorrowful: for he had great possessions.

Then said Jesus unto his disciples, Verily I say unto you, That a rich man shall hardly enter into the kingdom of heaven.

And again I say unto you, It is easier for a camel to go through the eye of a needle, than for a rich man to enter into the kingdom of God.

When his disciples heard it, they were exceedingly amazed, saying, Who then can be saved?

But Jesus beheld them, and said unto them, With men this is impossible; but with God all things are possible.

The story of Jesus teaching the rich young ruler is a story about a *one*—because the worth of souls is great in the sight of God.

JESUS HEALS THE SEVERED EAR OF THE SERVANT OF THE HIGH PRIEST (LUKE 22:48-51)

But Jesus said unto him, Judas, betrayest thou the Son of man with a kiss?

When they which were about him saw what would follow, they said unto him, Lord, shall we smite with the sword?

And one of them smote the servant of the high priest, and cut off his right ear.

And Jesus answered and said, Suffer ye thus far. And he touched his ear, and healed him.

The story of Jesus healing the severed ear of the servant of the high priest is a story about a *one*—because the worth of souls is great in the sight of God.

JESUS TEACHES PILATE (JOHN 18:33-38)

Then Pilate entered into the judgment hall again, and called Jesus, and said unto him, Art thou the King of the Jews?

Jesus answered him, Sayest thou this thing of thyself, or did others tell it thee of me?

Pilate answered, Am I a Jew? Thine own nation and the chief priests have delivered thee unto me: what hast thou done?

Jesus answered, My kingdom is not of this world: if my kingdom were of this world, then would my servants fight, that I should not be delivered to the Jews: but now is my kingdom not from hence.

Pilate therefore said unto him, Art thou a king then? Jesus answered, Thou sayest that I am a king. To this end was I born, and for this cause came I into the world, that I should bear witness unto the truth. Every one that is of the truth heareth my voice.

Pilate saith unto him, What is truth? And when he had said this, he went out again unto the Jews, and saith unto them, I find in him no fault at all.

The story of Jesus teaching Pilate is a story about a *one*—because the worth of souls is great in the sight of God.

JESUS SPEAKS TO THE THIEF FROM THE CROSS (LUKE 23:39-43)

And one of the malefactors which were hanged railed on him, saying, If thou be Christ, save thyself and us.

But the other answering rebuked him, saying,

Dost not thou fear God, seeing thou art in the same condemnation?

And we indeed justly; for we receive the due reward of our deeds: but this man hath done nothing amiss.

And he said unto Jesus, Lord, remember me when thou comest into thy kingdom.

And Jesus said unto him, Verily I say unto thee, To day shalt thou be with me in paradise.

The story of Jesus speaking to the thief from the cross is a story about a *one*—because the worth of souls is great in the sight of God.

JESUS SPEAKS TO HIS MOTHER FROM THE CROSS (JOHN 19:25-27)

Now there stood by the cross of Jesus his mother, and his mother's sister, Mary the wife of Cleophas, and Mary Magdalene.

When Jesus therefore saw his mother, and the disciple standing by, whom he loved, he saith unto his mother, Woman, behold thy son!

Then saith he to the disciple, Behold thy mother! And from that hour that disciple took her unto his own home.

The story of Jesus speaking to His mother from the cross is a story about a *one*—because the worth of souls is great in the sight of God.

JESUS APPEARS TO MARY MAGDALENE (JOHN 20:11-18)

But Mary stood without at the sepulchre weeping: and as she wept, she stooped down, and looked into the sepulchre,

And seeth two angels in white sitting, the one at the head, and the other at the feet, where the body of Jesus had lain.

And they say unto her, Woman, why weepest thou? She saith unto them, Because they have taken away my Lord, and I know not where they have laid him.

And when she had thus said, she turned herself back, and saw Jesus standing, and knew not that it was Jesus.

Jesus saith unto her, Woman, why weepest thou? whom seekest thou? She, supposing him to be the gardener, saith unto him, Sir, if thou have borne him hence, tell me where thou hast laid him, and I will take him away.

Jesus saith unto her, Mary. She turned herself, and saith unto him, Rabboni; which is to say, Master.

> Jesus saith unto her, Touch me not; for I am not yet ascended to my Father: but go to my brethren, and say unto them, I ascend unto my Father, and your Father; and to my God, and your God.
>
> Mary Magdalene came and told the disciples that she had seen the Lord, and that he had spoken these things unto her.

The story of Jesus appearing to Mary Magdalene is a story about a *one*—because the worth of souls is great in the sight of God.

JESUS APPEARS TO AND TEACHES TWO DISCIPLES ON THE ROAD TO EMMAUS (LUKE 24:13–35)

> And, behold, two of them went that same day to a village called Emmaus, which was from Jerusalem about threescore furlongs.
>
> And they talked together of all these things which had happened.
>
> And it came to pass, that, while they communed together and reasoned, Jesus himself drew near, and went with them.
>
> But their eyes were holden that they should not know him.
>
> And he said unto them, What manner of

communications are these that ye have one to an-other, as ye walk, and are sad?

And the one of them, whose name was Cleopas, answering said unto him, Art thou only a stranger in Jerusalem, and hast not known the things which are come to pass there in these days?

And he said unto them, What things? And they said unto him, Concerning Jesus of Nazareth, which was a prophet mighty in deed and word before God and all the people:

And how the chief priests and our rulers delivered him to be condemned to death, and have crucified him.

But we trusted that it had been he which should have redeemed Israel: and beside all this, to day is the third day since these things were done.

Yea, and certain women also of our company made us astonished, which were early at the sepulchre;

And when they found not his body, they came, saying, that they had also seen a vision of angels, which said that he was alive.

And certain of them which were with us went to the sepulchre, and found it even so as the women had said: but him they saw not.

Then he said unto them, O fools, and slow of heart to believe all that the prophets have spoken:

Ought not Christ to have suffered these things, and to enter into his glory?

And beginning at Moses and all the prophets, he expounded unto them in all the scriptures the things concerning himself.

And they drew nigh unto the village, whither they went: and he made as though he would have gone further.

But they constrained him, saying, Abide with us: for it is toward evening, and the day is far spent. And he went in to tarry with them.

And it came to pass, as he sat at meat with them, he took bread, and blessed it, and brake, and gave to them.

And their eyes were opened, and they knew him; and he vanished out of their sight.

And they said one to another, Did not our heart burn within us, while he talked with us by the way, and while he opened to us the scriptures?

And they rose up the same hour, and returned to Jerusalem, and found the eleven gathered together, and them that were with them,

> Saying, The Lord is risen indeed, and hath appeared to Simon.
>
> And they told what things were done in the way, and how he was known of them in breaking of bread.

The story of Jesus appearing to and teaching two disciples on the road to Emmaus is a story about two *ones*—because the worth of souls is great in the sight of God.

JESUS APPEARS TO AND TEACHES THOMAS (JOHN 20:24-29)

> But Thomas, one of the twelve, called Didymus, was not with them when Jesus came.
>
> The other disciples therefore said unto him, We have seen the Lord. But he said unto them, Except I shall see in his hands the print of the nails, and put my finger into the print of the nails, and thrust my hand into his side, I will not believe.
>
> And after eight days again his disciples were within, and Thomas with them: then came Jesus, the doors being shut, and stood in the midst, and said, Peace be unto you.
>
> Then saith he to Thomas, Reach hither thy finger, and behold my hands; and reach hither thy hand, and thrust it into my side: and be not faithless, but believing.

And Thomas answered and said unto him, My Lord and my God.

Jesus saith unto him, Thomas, because thou hast seen me, thou hast believed: blessed are they that have not seen, and yet have believed.

The story of Jesus appearing to and teaching Thomas is a story about a *one*—because the worth of souls is great in the sight of God.

JESUS TEACHES PETER TO FEED HIS SHEEP (JOHN 21:15-17)

So when they had dined, Jesus saith to Simon Peter, Simon, son of Jonas, lovest thou me more than these? He saith unto him, Yea, Lord; thou knowest that I love thee. He saith unto him, Feed my lambs.

He saith to him again the second time, Simon, son of Jonas, lovest thou me? He saith unto him, Yea, Lord; thou knowest that I love thee. He saith unto him, Feed my sheep.

He saith unto him the third time, Simon, son of Jonas, lovest thou me? Peter was grieved because he said unto him the third time, Lovest thou me? And he said unto him, Lord, thou knowest all things; thou knowest that I love thee. Jesus saith unto him, Feed my sheep.

The story of Jesus teaching Peter to feed His lambs is not a story about a flock. Rather, it is a story about millions and tens of millions and hundreds of millions of *ones*—because the worth of souls is great in the sight of God.

SUMMARY

President Howard W. Hunter summarized in beautiful simplicity the responsibility that rests upon each of us to emulate the character of the Master.

"To the very end of his mortal life Jesus was demonstrating the grandeur of his spirit and the magnitude of his strength. He was not, even at this late hour, selfishly engrossed with his own sorrows or contemplating the impending pain. He was anxiously attending to the present and future needs of his beloved followers. He knew their own safety, individually and as a church, lay only in their unconditional love one for another. His entire energies seem to have been directed toward their needs, thus teaching by example what he was teaching by precept. He gave them words of comfort and commandment and caution" ("His Final Hours," *Ensign,* May 1974).

"What a marvelous example for us to follow! Even in the midst of great personal sorrow and pain, our Exemplar reached out to bless others. . . . His was not a life focused on the things he did not have. It was a life of reaching out in service to others" (Howard W. Hunter, "The Church Is for All People," *Ensign,* June 1989).

President Thomas S. Monson admonished, "Never let a problem to be solved become more important than a person to be loved" ("Finding Joy in the Journey," *Ensign,* November 2008). His simple statement clarifies concisely the importance of emulating the character of Christ and employing His pattern of ministering *one by one*—because the worth of souls is great in the sight of God.

> *One by one, one by one.*
> *Jesus, the Father's Beloved Son*
> *One by one, one by one*
> *From the beginning said, "Thy will be done."*
> *Jesus Christ came to earth to fulfill God's plan,*
> *For He alone could atone as Savior of man.*
> *The Lord blessed and beckoned them, "Come unto me,"*
> *And willingly sacrificed to set us free.*
> *One by one, one by one.*
> *He suffered for us and victory won.*
> *One by one, one by one.*
> *We marvel at all His love has done,*
> *One by one.*

Questions to Consider

1. What can and should I do in my life to better follow the Savior's example of selflessly ministering *one by one*?

2. How does increasing my understanding about the worth of souls in the sight of God affect my motives, my heart, and my behavior?

3. What can and should I do in my life to discern and appreciate more fully the spiritual worth of individuals?

My Own Questions to Consider

1. _____

_____

2. _____

_____

3. _____

_____

Scriptures Related to What I Am Learning

_____

_____

_____

CHAPTER 3

ONE BY ONE AND THE BOOK OF MORMON

The Book of Mormon is another testament of Jesus Christ, focusing upon the life and divine mission of the Master. This sacred volume of scripture describes the ministry and teaches the doctrine of Christ with clarity, using understandable language. The writings of prophets such as Nephi, Jacob, Alma, Mormon, Moroni, and others testify of the Word who was with God, and who was God, and by whom all things were made (see John 1:1). As Nephi proclaimed, "We are made alive in Christ because of our faith; . . . And we talk of Christ, we rejoice in Christ, we preach of Christ, we prophesy of Christ, and we write according to our prophecies, that our children may know to what source they may look for a remission of their sins" (2 Nephi 25:25–26).

The convincing and converting power of the Book of Mormon results from both a central focus upon the Lord Jesus Christ and the inspired plainness and clarity of its teachings. Nephi declared, "My soul delighteth in plainness unto my people, that they may learn" (2 Nephi 25:4). The root word *plain* in this verse does not refer to things that are ordinary or simple; rather, it denotes instruction that is clear and easily understood.

The unique combination of these two factors—a central emphasis on the Savior and the plainness of the teachings—powerfully invites the confirming witness of the third member of the Godhead, even the Holy Ghost. Consequently, the Book of Mormon speaks to the mind, the spirit, and the heart of the reader like no other volume of scripture.

No other scriptural source provides more knowledge about or describes so sublimely and clearly the Father's plan of happiness and the infinite Atonement of the Lord Jesus Christ. Interestingly, the word *atonement* in any of its forms is used only once in the King James Version of the New Testament. By comparison, in the Book of Mormon it appears thirty-nine times. Other plain and precious truths such as the Resurrection, the nature of fallen man, the importance of moral agency, and the relationship between justice and mercy are presented with clarity and power. In a world that grows ever more secular and confused about the identity and mission of Jesus the Christ, the Book of Mormon is a singular source of plain, precious, and eternally satisfying answers—"to the convincing of the Jew and Gentile that Jesus is the Christ" (Book of Mormon, title page).

EXAMPLES OF ONE BY ONE IN THE BOOK OF MORMON

We can learn much in the Book of Mormon: Another Testament of Jesus Christ about the Savior and His pattern of ministering *one by one.* The latter-day purpose, power, and relevance of this sacred volume of scripture help us to see with new eyes and to hear with new ears (see Doctrine and Covenants 136:32).

The exact phrase *one by one* is used six times in the Book of Mormon. Four of the references are in 3 Nephi (11:15; 17:21; 18:36; 28:1), one is in the book of Helaman (9:18), and one is in the book of Ether (3:6).

The phrase *one by one* is used in Helaman to describe the efforts of five judges to defend the prophet Nephi against a false accusation of having committed a crime; it has no relevance to the primary purpose of this chapter. By contrast, four of the six instances of the phrase *one by one* are found in the chapters in 3 Nephi describing the personal visitation and ministry of the resurrected Lord among the Nephites. The Lord is also central in the interaction with the brother of Jared detailed in the book of Ether.

The focus in this chapter will be upon the five specific examples contained in the Book of Mormon of the Savior and His servants ministering and blessing *one by one.*

AT THE TEMPLE IN THE LAND OF BOUNTIFUL (3 NEPHI 11:6–17)

And behold, the third time they did understand the voice which they heard; and it said unto them:

Behold my Beloved Son, in whom I am well pleased, in whom I have glorified my name—hear ye him.

And it came to pass, as they understood they cast their eyes up again towards heaven; and behold, they saw a Man descending out of heaven; and he was clothed in a white robe; and he came down and stood in the midst of them; and the eyes of the whole multitude were turned upon him, and they durst not open their mouths, even one to another, and wist not what it meant, for they thought it was an angel that had appeared unto them.

And it came to pass that he stretched forth his hand and spake unto the people, saying:

Behold, I am Jesus Christ, whom the prophets testified shall come into the world.

And behold, I am the light and the life of the world; and I have drunk out of that bitter cup which the Father hath given me, and have glorified the Father in taking upon me the sins of the world, in the which I have suffered the will of the Father in all things from the beginning.

And it came to pass that when Jesus had spoken these words the whole multitude fell to the earth; for they remembered that it had been prophesied among them that Christ should show himself unto them after his ascension into heaven.

And it came to pass that the Lord spake unto them saying:

Arise and come forth unto me, that ye may thrust your hands into my side, and also that ye may feel the prints of the nails in my hands and in my feet, that ye may know that I am the God of Israel, and the God of the whole earth, and have been slain for the sins of the world.

And it came to pass that the multitude went forth, and thrust their hands into his side, and did feel the prints of the nails in his hands and in his feet; and this they did do, going forth *one by one* until they had all gone forth, and did see with their eyes and did feel with their hands, and did know of a surety and did bear record, that it was he, of whom it was written by the prophets, that should come.

And when they had all gone forth and had

witnessed for themselves, they did cry out with one accord, saying:

Hosanna! Blessed be the name of the Most High God! And they did fall down at the feet of Jesus, and did worship him.

The story in the Book of Mormon about the multitude going forth to thrust their hands into the Savior's side and to feel the prints in His hands and in His feet is a story about 2,500 *ones*—because the worth of souls is great in the sight of God.

I invite you to now consider the remarkable background and context of this sacred visitation. In the land of Zarahemla a few years before the birth of the Savior, Samuel the Lamanite came among the people to preach repentance and prophesy of Christ. Please try to imagine that you are ten years old and a member of the multitude listening to a prophet of God foretell future events.

Samuel declared:

Behold, I give unto you a sign; for five years more cometh, and behold, then cometh the Son of God to redeem all those who shall believe on his name.

And behold, this will I give unto you for a sign at the time of his coming; for behold, there shall be great lights in heaven, insomuch that in the night before he cometh there shall be no darkness, insomuch that it shall appear unto man as if it was day.

Therefore, there shall be one day and a night and a day, as if it were one day and there were no night; and this shall be unto you for a sign. . . .

And behold, there shall a new star arise . . . ; and this also shall be a sign unto you. (Helaman 14:2–5)

THE SAVIOR'S BIRTH

As time passed, "the prophecies of the prophets began to be fulfilled more fully; for there began to be greater signs and greater miracles wrought among the people" (3 Nephi 1:4).

Imagine five years have passed and you are now approximately fifteen years old. You can recall clearly the prophecies of Samuel as you consider the present circumstances in which you live.

But there were some who began to say that the time was past for the words to be fulfilled, which were spoken by Samuel, the Lamanite.

And they began to rejoice over their brethren, saying: Behold the time is past, and the words of Samuel are not fulfilled; therefore, your joy and your faith concerning this thing hath been vain.

And it came to pass that they did make a great uproar throughout the land; and the people who believed began to be very sorrowful, lest by any means those things which had been spoken might not come to pass.

But behold, they did watch steadfastly for that day and that night and that day which should be as one day as if there were no night, that they might know that their faith had not been vain.

Now it came to pass that there was a day set apart by the unbelievers, that all those who believed in those traditions should be put to death except the sign should come to pass, which had been given by Samuel the prophet. (3 Nephi 1:5–9)

Can we even begin to understand what it might have been like to await the sign of His coming and also face the dire deadline of death? Would you and I stand firm and steadfast in the faith, or would we waver and shrink?

Then, indeed, the sign of Christ's birth foretold by Samuel was given. In a climate of religious persecution and at the tender age of approximately fifteen, you marveled one evening as the sun went down but there was no darkness.

And the people began to be astonished because there was no darkness when the night came. . . .

And they began to know that the Son of God

must shortly appear; yea . . . , all the people . . . were so exceedingly astonished that they fell to the earth. . . .

And it came to pass that there was no darkness in all that night, but it was as light as though it was mid-day. And it came to pass that the sun did rise in the morning again . . . ; and they knew that it was the day that the Lord should be born, because of the sign which had been given.

And it had come to pass, yea, all things, every whit, according to the words of the prophets.

And it came to pass also that a new star did appear, according to the word. (3 Nephi 1:15, 17, 19–21)

The day Jesus was born was a day of deliverance for the believers in the New World. Light as the sign of the Savior's birth literally saved their lives.

THE SAVIOR'S DEATH AND RESURRECTION

Now imagine that more than thirty years have passed and you are approaching fifty years of age. You still can remember vividly the teachings of Samuel and your experiences as a teenager when the sign of the Lord's birth was given.

One of the signs of Christ's death foretold by Samuel was three days of intense darkness (see Helaman 14:27; 3 Nephi 8:3).

> And it came to pass that there was thick darkness upon all the face of the land, insomuch that the inhabitants thereof who had not fallen could feel the vapor of darkness;
>
> And there could be no light, because of the darkness, neither candles, neither torches; neither could there be fire kindled . . . , so that there could not be any light at all;
>
> And there was not any light seen, neither fire, nor glimmer, neither the sun, nor the moon, nor the stars, for so great were the mists of darkness which were upon the face of the land.
>
> And it came to pass that it did last for the space of three days that there was no light seen. (3 Nephi 8:20–23)

What might it have been like to experience those three days of indescribable darkness and then, a short time later, gather with the multitude of 2,500 people at the temple in the land of Bountiful? Can you envision the majesty of the moment as the Savior descended from the heavens and declared, "Behold, I am Jesus Christ . . . I am the *light* and the life of the world"?

To this special assembly at the temple, two of the first words the Savior used to describe Himself were "the light." Samuel predicted a sign of light. The sign of light was given at the Savior's birth. For the people in the assembled multitude, terrible darkness and fear had been dissipated by the true light, even Jesus Christ.

This account in the Book of Mormon helps us to learn and more fully understand that Jesus Christ is the "light which shineth in darkness" (see Doctrine and Covenants 10:57–61).

And then try to imagine what it might have been like to hear His voice and receive this invitation: "Arise and come forth unto me, that ye may thrust your hands into my side, and also that ye may feel the prints of the nails in my hands and in my feet, that ye may know that I am the God of Israel, and the God of the whole earth, and have been slain for the sins of the world" (3 Nephi 11:14).

This invitation was not restricted to a select minority. This invitation was not given to a few representative participants who could then testify to the assembled multitude. Rather, this invitation was extended to every individual gathered at the temple in the land of Bountiful. The invitation was to come out of the collective congregation and have an experience with the Redeemer as a *one*.

And it came to pass that the multitude went forth, and thrust their hands into his side, and did feel the prints of the nails in his hands and in his feet; and this they did do, going forth *one by one* until they had all gone forth, and did see with their eyes and did feel with their hands, and did know of a surety and did bear record, that it was he, of whom it was written by the prophets, that should come.

And when they had all gone forth and had witnessed for themselves, they did cry out with one accord, saying:

Hosanna! Blessed be the name of the Most High God! And they did fall down at the feet of Jesus, and did worship him. (3 Nephi 11:15–17)

Please consider one additional and spiritually important aspect of this "crowning event" recorded in the Book of Mormon (see Book of Mormon, introduction). The multitude totaled 2,500 souls, and the record states that "all of them did see and hear, every man for himself" (3 Nephi 17:25). If each person were given fifteen seconds to approach the resurrected Lord, thrust his or her hand into His side, and feel the prints of the nails, more than ten hours would be required to complete the process.

I know of no greater example and no more powerful and enduring illustration of the Savior's individual concern for the sons and daughters of God than the account of His personal ministry contained in the Book of Mormon. In this additional testament of Him and His divinity, He ministers *one by one* and highlights a powerful pattern for accomplishing His Father's eternal work.

THE LORD BLESSES THE CHILDREN (3 NEPHI 17:11-25)

And it came to pass that he commanded that their little children should be brought.

So they brought their little children and set them down upon the ground round about him, and Jesus stood in the midst; and the multitude gave way till they had all been brought unto him.

And it came to pass that when they had all been brought, and Jesus stood in the midst, he commanded the multitude that they should kneel down upon the ground.

And it came to pass that when they had knelt upon the ground, Jesus groaned within himself, and said: Father, I am troubled because of the wickedness of the people of the house of Israel.

And when he had said these words, he himself also knelt upon the earth; and behold he prayed unto the Father, and the things which he prayed cannot be written, and the multitude did bear record who heard him.

And after this manner do they bear record: The eye hath never seen, neither hath the ear heard, before, so great and marvelous things as we saw and heard Jesus speak unto the Father;

And no tongue can speak, neither can there be written by any man, neither can the hearts of men conceive so great and marvelous things as we both saw and heard Jesus speak; and no one can conceive of the joy which filled our souls at the time we heard him pray for us unto the Father.

And it came to pass that when Jesus had made an end of praying unto the Father, he arose; but so great was the joy of the multitude that they were overcome.

And it came to pass that Jesus spake unto them, and bade them arise.

And they arose from the earth, and he said unto them: Blessed are ye because of your faith. And now behold, my joy is full.

And when he had said these words, he wept, and the multitude bare record of it, and he took their little children, *one by one,* and blessed them, and prayed unto the Father for them.

And when he had done this he wept again;

And he spake unto the multitude, and said unto them: Behold your little ones.

And as they looked to behold they cast their eyes towards heaven, and they saw the heavens open, and they saw angels descending out of heaven as it were in the midst of fire; and they came down and encircled those little ones about, and they were encircled about with fire; and the angels did minister unto them.

And the multitude did see and hear and bear record; and they know that their record is true for they all of them did see and hear, every man for himself; and they were in number about two thousand and five hundred souls; and they did consist of men, women, and children.

The story in the Book of Mormon about the Savior blessing the children is a story about many *ones*—because the worth of souls is great in the sight of God.

The account does not indicate how many children were included among the 2,500—perhaps a few hundred. And how long might it have taken for Jesus to take each child and personally bless him or her? Undoubtedly hours were devoted to these *one-by-one* blessings. And the blessing of the children occurred on the same day of and after the invitation from Jesus for the people to come forth individually to feel the prints in His hands and feet and the wound in His side.

Again, the Savior's continuous love and concern for individuals is manifested in this sequence of tender experiences.

JESUS TOUCHES HIS DISCIPLES (3 NEPHI 18:36-39)

And it came to pass that when Jesus had made an end of these sayings, he touched with his hand the disciples whom he had chosen, *one by one,* even until he had touched them all, and spake unto them as he touched them.

And the multitude heard not the words which he spake, therefore they did not bear record; but the disciples bare record that he gave them power to give the Holy Ghost. And I will show unto you hereafter that this record is true.

And it came to pass that when Jesus had touched them all, there came a cloud and overshadowed the multitude that they could not see Jesus.

And while they were overshadowed he departed from them, and ascended into heaven. And the disciples saw and did bear record that he ascended again into heaven.

The story in the Book of Mormon about the Savior touching His disciples is a story about twelve *ones*—because the worth of souls is great in the sight of God.

JESUS SPEAKS TO HIS DISCIPLES (3 NEPHI 28:1-12)

And it came to pass when Jesus had said these words, he spake unto his disciples, *one by one,* saying unto them: What is it that ye desire of me, after that I am gone to the Father?

And they all spake, save it were three, saying: We desire that after we have lived unto the age of man, that our ministry, wherein thou hast called us, may have an end, that we may speedily come unto thee in thy kingdom.

And he said unto them: Blessed are ye because ye desired this thing of me; therefore, after that ye are seventy and two years old ye shall come unto me in my kingdom; and with me ye shall find rest.

And when he had spoken unto them, he turned himself unto the three, and said unto them: What will ye that I should do unto you, when I am gone unto the Father?

And they sorrowed in their hearts, for they durst not speak unto him the thing which they desired.

And he said unto them: Behold, I know your thoughts, and ye have desired the thing which John, my beloved, who was with me in my ministry, before that I was lifted up by the Jews, desired of me.

Therefore, more blessed are ye, for ye shall never taste of death; but ye shall live to behold all the doings of the Father unto the children of men, even until all things shall be fulfilled according to the will of the Father, when I shall come in my glory with the powers of heaven.

And ye shall never endure the pains of death; but when I shall come in my glory ye shall be changed in the twinkling of an eye from mortality to immortality; and then shall ye be blessed in the kingdom of my Father.

And again, ye shall not have pain while ye shall dwell in the flesh, neither sorrow save it be for the sins of the world; and all this will I do because of the thing which ye have desired of me, for ye have desired that ye might bring the souls of men unto me, while the world shall stand.

And for this cause ye shall have fulness of joy; and ye shall sit down in the kingdom of my Father; yea, your joy shall be full, even as the Father hath given me fulness of joy; and ye shall be even as I am, and I am even as the Father; and the Father and I are one;

And the Holy Ghost beareth record of the Father and me; and the Father giveth the Holy Ghost unto the children of men, because of me.

And it came to pass that when Jesus had spoken these words, he touched every one of them with his finger save it were the three who were to tarry, and then he departed.

The story in the Book of Mormon about the Savior speaking with His disciples is a story about twelve *ones*—because the worth of souls is great in the sight of God.

The individual nature of the interaction and experiences between the Savior and His twelve disciples described in chapters 18 and 28 of 3 Nephi is most instructive. Significantly, the Lord invited each man to express his heartfelt desire. And equally significantly, the disciples did not all have the same yearning. The Savior respected and honored their distinctive requests and did not in any way cause His followers to feel as though they needed to pursue identical personal objectives.

Jesus sensed the reluctance of three disciples to disclose to Him their hope to continue in their ministry until the time of His Second Coming. He instructed, reassured, and blessed according to their individual needs and wants. The Savior set the example for those whom He authorized to go forth and minister *one by one* by ministering to them *one by one*.

THE BROTHER OF JARED (ETHER 3:1–6)

And it came to pass that the brother of Jared, (now the number of the vessels which had been prepared was eight) went forth unto the mount, which they called the mount Shelem, because of its exceeding height, and did molten out of a rock sixteen small stones; and they were white and clear, even as transparent glass; and he did carry them in his hands upon the top of the mount, and cried again unto the Lord, saying:

O Lord, thou hast said that we must be encompassed about by the floods. Now behold, O Lord, and do not be angry with thy servant because of his weakness before thee; for we know that thou art holy and dwellest in the heavens, and that we are unworthy before thee; because of the fall our natures have become evil continually; nevertheless, O Lord, thou hast given us a commandment that we must call upon thee, that from thee we may receive according to our desires.

Behold, O Lord, thou hast smitten us because of our iniquity, and hast driven us forth, and for these many years we have been in the wilderness; nevertheless, thou hast been merciful unto us. O Lord, look upon me in pity, and turn away thine anger from this thy people, and suffer not that they shall go forth across this raging deep in darkness; but behold these things which I have molten out of the rock.

And I know, O Lord, that thou hast all power, and can do whatsoever thou wilt for the benefit of man; therefore touch these stones, O Lord, with thy finger, and prepare them that they may shine forth in darkness; and they shall shine forth unto us in the vessels which we have prepared, that we may have light while we shall cross the sea.

Behold, O Lord, thou canst do this. We know that thou art able to show forth great power, which looks small unto the understanding of men.

And it came to pass that when the brother of Jared had said these words, behold, the Lord stretched forth his hand and touched the stones *one by one* with his finger. And the veil was taken from off the eyes of the brother of Jared, and he saw the finger of the Lord; and it was as the finger of a man, like unto flesh and blood; and the brother of Jared fell down before the Lord, for he was struck with fear.

The story in the Book of Mormon about the brother of Jared and the stones is also a story about *ones*—because the worth of souls is great in the sight of God.

I invite you to consider this question: Why were the sixteen stones touched *one by one?* Why not simply illuminate all sixteen stones at the same time? Why take the time to touch each stone *one by one?*

Please consider two possible interpretations of this experience. I present these alternative explanations as impetus to stimulate the spiritual process of asking, seeking, knocking, and pondering, and not as a statement of doctrine.

One interpretation is that the brother of Jared immediately saw the finger of the Lord touch sequentially each of the sixteen stones. This explanation, however, appears to be contrary to a principle emphasized throughout the scriptures—that we receive no witness until after the trial of our faith (see Ether 12:6).

A second interpretation is that the veil was not necessarily removed immediately as the finger of the Lord touched the first stone.

The brother of Jared prayed with great faith and with the "assurance of things hoped for" (JST, Hebrews 11:1). Imagine that the first stone was illuminated, but the brother of Jared did not yet see the Lord's finger. What would happen to his faith? Surely it would increase and become stronger because of the "evidence of things not seen" (Hebrews 11:1). Then imagine a second stone was illuminated, without the brother of Jared yet seeing the Lord's finger. His faith would have been further strengthened. The lighting of each successive stone would be an ongoing cycle of "exercising a particle of faith," "experimenting upon the word," and ultimately receiving "a perfect knowledge" (see Alma 32:27–34).

Thus, a second way of interpreting this episode is that perhaps after many or even all of the stones were illuminated, the veil was then removed and the brother of Jared saw the finger of the Lord.

The experience of the brother of Jared may be considered a type and a shadow for our own service in our families and in the

Church. The stones may be symbols for and represent people who are touched by the Lord and illuminated *one by one.*

As a priesthood leader, I have worked with sin-sick souls who had replaced the light of righteousness in their countenances with the darkness of transgression and guilt. Gratefully, through the process of sincere repentance, many of those individuals were touched by the finger of the Lord and changed by the power of His infinite and eternal Atonement. The light in their souls gradually returned, "line upon line, precept upon precept" (2 Nephi 28:30). And as we serve in our families and minister to the sons and daughters of God with all of our heart, might, mind, and strength, we also are blessed to see the "evidence of things not seen" (Hebrews 11:1).

We may not see the literal finger of the Lord touch the hearts of the people we serve. But we do see repentant souls partake of the precious white fruit and relish the delicious taste of the Atonement of Jesus Christ in their lives. They are touched, healed, and blessed *one by one.* What once was dark because of sin is light again because of the Savior's Atonement. Jesus indeed is "the light which shineth in darkness" (Doctrine and Covenants 6:21).

SUMMARY

One of the key episodes in the Book of Mormon is Lehi's dream. The central feature in Lehi's dream is the tree of life, which is a representation of "the love of God" (1 Nephi 11:22).

The birth, life, and atoning sacrifice of the Lord Jesus Christ are the greatest manifestations of God's love for His children. "For God so loved the world, that he gave his only begotten Son, that whosoever believeth in him should not perish, but have everlasting life" (John 3:16). The tree can be considered as a representation of Christ.

The central Book of Mormon invitation to "come unto Christ, and be perfected in him" (Moroni 10:32) can be linked to the symbolism of pressing forward with steadfastness along the strait and narrow path and partaking of the fruit of the tree. One way of thinking about the fruit is as a symbol for the blessings of the Savior's Atonement. Lehi described the fruit as "most sweet, above all that I ever before tasted. Yea, and I beheld that the fruit thereof was white, to exceed all the whiteness that I had ever seen" (1 Nephi 8:11).

Interestingly, an individual can obtain the path that leads to the tree and the fruit only by entering through the gate—even the ordinances of baptism by immersion for the remission of sins and laying on of hands for the gift of the Holy Ghost. "For the gate by which ye should enter is repentance and baptism by water; and then cometh a remission of your sins by fire and by the Holy Ghost" (2 Nephi 31:17).

Pressing forward to and partaking of the fruit of the tree may represent the receiving of additional ordinances and covenants whereby the Savior's Atonement can become fully efficacious in our lives. The fruit is "desirable to make one happy" (1 Nephi 8:10) and produces great joy and the desire to share that joy with others.

Please now consider the sobering significance of the implications that arise from Lehi's vision. To come unto the Savior, an individual *must* first pass through the gate of baptism and receive the gift of the Holy Ghost—and then continue to press forward along the path of ordinances, covenants, and faithfulness that leads to the Savior and the blessings of His Atonement (see 2 Nephi 31). Without the ordinances and associated covenants, an individual cannot receive all of the blessings made possible through the Lord's infinite and eternal atoning sacrifice (see Alma 34:10–14).

Steady and sustained progress along the strait and narrow path toward the tree is the course of life we should pursue that is in accordance with God's will. Lehi's dream specifically identifies the course we should follow, the challenges we will encounter, and the spiritual resources available to assist us in coming unto the Savior. Pressing forward on the strait and narrow path is what He would have us do. Tasting the fruit of the tree and becoming deeply "converted unto the Lord" (Alma 23:6) are the blessings He yearns for us to receive.

Pressing forward along the strait and narrow path is a journey every individual must make for himself or herself. Indeed, it is a *one-by-one* journey. We may travel with our families, friends, and other people who will support and encourage us. Ultimately, however, every person individually receives, remembers, and honors sacred ordinances and covenants and strives to become a devoted disciple. This personal spiritual responsibility cannot be delegated or shared.

The scriptures declare that on a future day *every* knee shall bow and *every* tongue confess that Jesus is the Christ (see Romans 14:11; Mosiah 27:31). The Final Judgment will occur after the Resurrection. God, through Jesus Christ, will judge each person to determine the eternal glory he or she will receive. This judgment will be based on each person's obedience to God's commands, including his or her acceptance of the atoning sacrifice of Jesus Christ. The pattern of *one by one* will again be employed as we are held accountable for the exercise of our moral agency in mortality.

> Therefore, prepare ye the way of the Lord, for the time is at hand that all men shall reap a reward of their works, according to that which they have been—if they have been righteous they shall reap the salvation of their souls, according to the power and deliverance of Jesus Christ; and if they have been evil they shall reap the damnation of their souls, according to the power and captivation of the devil. (Alma 9:28)
>
> Wherefore, we shall have a perfect knowledge of

all our guilt, and our uncleanness, and our nakedness; and the righteous shall have a perfect knowledge of their enjoyment, and their righteousness, being clothed with purity, yea, even with the robe of righteousness.

And it shall come to pass that when all men shall have passed from this first death unto life, insomuch as they have become immortal, they must appear before the judgment-seat of the Holy One of Israel; and then cometh the judgment, and then must they be judged according to the holy judgment of God. (2 Nephi 9:14–15)

O, my beloved brethren, turn away from your sins; shake off the chains of him that would bind you fast; come unto that God who is the rock of your salvation.

Prepare your souls for that glorious day when justice shall be administered unto the righteous, even the day of judgment, that ye may not shrink with awful fear; that ye may not remember your awful guilt in perfectness, and be constrained to exclaim: Holy, holy are thy judgments, O Lord God Almighty—but I know my guilt; I transgressed thy law, and my transgressions are mine; and the devil hath obtained me, that I am a prey to his awful misery. (2 Nephi 9:45–46)

Our loving and living Savior pleads, beckons, and invites us *one by one*—because the worth of souls is great in the sight of God.

"Yea, verily I say unto you, if ye will come unto me ye shall have eternal life. Behold, mine arm of mercy is extended towards you, and whosoever will come, him will I receive; and blessed are those who come unto me" (3 Nephi 9:14).

> *One by one, one by one.*
>> *Multitudes gathered and saw Him come.*
> *One by one, one by one.*
>> *Each heard a voice declare, "Behold My Son."*
> *Jesus Christ came and stood in the midst of them.*
>> *They fell to the earth in great reverence for Him.*
> *The Lord bid, "Arise, and come forth unto me."*
>> *With hands they did feel and with eyes they did see.*
> *One by one, one by one.*
>> *Each knew and bore record, He is our Lord.*
> *One by one, one by one.*
>> *They cried "Hosanna" with one accord,*
> *One by one.*
>
> *One by one, one by one.*
>> *Christ looked around Him and saw their tears.*
> *One by one, one by one.*
>> *In His compassion, He calmed their fears.*

Jesus Christ healed each one brought forth unto Him.

Then He blessed each precious child and prayed for them.

The angels descended from heaven above,

Encircling those little ones; each felt His love.

One by one, one by one.

He intercedes for each daughter and son.

One by one, one by one.

Strength from His grace gives us power to become,

One by one.

Questions to Consider

1. What can and should I do to "treasure up continually" the lessons learned from studying the ministry of the Savior in the New Testament and the Book of Mormon?

2. How does increasing my understanding of the Lord's mortal ministry as recorded in the New Testament and the Book of Mormon affect my motives, my heart, and my behavior?

3. What can and should I do to recognize the "evidence of things not seen" in my own and others' lives and to become a worthy instrument in the hands of the Lord?

My Own Questions to Consider

1. _____

_____

2. _____

_____

3. _____

_____

Scriptures Related to What I Am Learning

_____

_____

_____

CHAPTER 4

ONE BY ONE AND THE WORK OF THE MINISTRY

I recently fulfilled an assignment in a Latin American country. My travels took my companions and me to cities both large and small, and we were blessed to meet with Latter-day Saints in many gatherings.

In one of the meetings, I spoke about the eternal importance of the Lord's latter-day work and emphasized the fact that we are not merely managing an organization or directing programs. Rather, our foremost responsibility is to reach out and serve our brothers and sisters *one by one*. In my message, I described several experiences in which I believed my assignments had taken me to places in the world so I could encounter and minister to specific individuals or families. And I indicated that such experiences are not restricted to General Authorities. All of us as members of the Lord's restored Church are tools in His hands to accomplish His work. Following the meeting, I greeted and shook hands with the members. My associates and I then were taken to a nearby airport so we could fly to another city and continue our assignment.

Early the next morning, we were scheduled to meet with and instruct approximately two hundred missionaries. As our vehicle pulled into the church parking lot, I noticed a man and a woman waiting outside near a front entrance to the chapel. I assumed they were a missionary couple or perhaps had provided transportation to the building for some of the missionaries. Quickly our car proceeded to the back of the building, and we were escorted into the chapel area and greeted the waiting missionaries. We were blessed to participate in an edifying session with faithful servants of the Lord.

We exited the building around 1:00 p.m. As we stepped outside, the woman I had noticed earlier in the morning at the entrance near the front of the building approached me and said something that, because of her accent and broken English, I could not understand. I asked her to repeat her comment, and I thought she said, "I think I a one." Again, I did not quite catch her meaning. I asked her to repeat her statement, and she again said, "I think I a one." The look on my face obviously revealed my confusion, and the woman continued. "Yesterday you talked Lord blesses one by one. I think I a one."

Only then did I realize that this good woman and her husband, in response to the message delivered the previous day, had traveled in their car a very great distance and waited outside the chapel all morning hoping we might have an opportunity to talk briefly together. My heart filled with love and compassion as I recognized more fully their faithfulness, desire, and sacrifice.

We spent several minutes discussing the challenge this man and woman were facing. I offered counsel and further explained that their bishop was in the best position to provide ongoing support and assistance. I explained the importance of the bishop's priesthood keys and how those keys would bless their lives. I expressed my love to this man and woman and reassured them that the Lord was aware of them as *ones* and as a couple. I promised they would be in my prayers.

I will never forget the expression of this humble and earnest sister, "I think I a one."

Obviously, the Lord cannot send General Authorities or general auxiliary leaders to minister to the individual needs of every member of His restored Church. A priesthood blessing by a worthy man serving faithfully as a home teacher is every bit as efficacious as a blessing from a General Authority. And inspired counsel from a bishop or stake president, acting in the authority of the priesthood keys he received at the time he was set apart, will bless the life of a member searching for direction and assurance. However, according to the Lord's will and timing and purposes, He does send His ordained servants to deliver messages and minister to individuals and families.

THE WORK OF THE MINISTRY

The work of the ministry is to do the work of the Lord on the earth—to represent the Lord among the people, to preach His gospel, and to administer by proper priesthood authority His saving and exalting ordinances. The chosen servants and appointed officers in the Church of Jesus Christ are put on earth by Him to conduct the work necessary for the salvation of mankind.

Each member of the Savior's restored Church also has a personal and *one-by-one* ministry to perform with family members, friends, and other Latter-day Saints. This individualized work of the ministry includes both fulfilling Church callings and assignments and performing simple acts of Christian and charitable service. People need not be authorized leaders in the Church to feel the responsibility of ministering to and blessing those with whom they interact.

The scriptures are replete with examples of the work of the ministry, as evidenced in the following selected verses.

JESUS CHRIST

And it came to pass that Jesus grew up with his brethren, and waxed strong, and waited upon the Lord for *the time of his ministry* to come.

And he served under his father, and he spake not as other men, neither could he be taught; for he needed not that any man should teach him.

And after many years, *the hour of his ministry* drew nigh. (JST, Matthew 3:24–26)

ABRAHAM

Behold, I will lead thee by my hand, and I will take thee, to put upon thee my name, even the Priesthood of thy father, and my power shall be over thee.

As it was with Noah so shall it be with thee; but *through thy ministry* my name shall be known in the earth forever, for I am thy God. (Abraham 1:18–19)

My name is Jehovah, and I know the end from the beginning; therefore my hand shall be over thee.

And I will make of thee a great nation, and I will bless thee above measure, and make thy name great among all nations, and thou shalt be a blessing unto thy seed after thee, that in their hands *they shall bear this ministry* and Priesthood unto all nations. (Abraham 2:8–9)

THE ANCIENT CHURCH OF JESUS CHRIST

And he gave some, apostles; and some, prophets; and some, evangelists; and some, pastors and teachers;

For the perfecting of the saints, for *the work of the ministry,* for the edifying of the body of Christ:

Till we all come in the unity of the faith, and of the knowledge of the Son of God, unto a perfect man, unto the measure of the stature of the fulness of Christ. (Ephesians 4:11–13)

ANCIENT APOSTLES

Then the twelve called the multitude of the disciples unto them, and said, It is not reason that we should leave the word of God, and serve tables.

Wherefore, brethren, look ye out among you seven men of honest report, full of the Holy Ghost and wisdom, whom we may appoint over this business.

But we will give ourselves continually to prayer, and *to the ministry of the word.* (Acts 6:2–4)

MORONI

An epistle of my father Mormon, written to me, Moroni; and it was written unto me soon after *my calling to the ministry.* And on this wise did he write unto me, saying:

My beloved son, Moroni, I rejoice exceedingly that your Lord Jesus Christ hath been mindful of you, and hath *called you to his ministry,* and to his holy work. (Moroni 8:1–2)

JOSEPH SMITH

And also with Peter, and James, and John, whom I have sent unto you, by whom I have ordained you and confirmed you to be apostles, and especial witnesses of my name, and bear *the keys of your ministry* and of the same things which I revealed unto them;

Unto whom I have committed the keys of my kingdom, and a dispensation of the gospel for the last times; and for the fulness of times, in the which I will gather together in one all things, both which are in heaven, and which are on earth. (Doctrine and Covenants 27:12–13)

For behold, I will be with him, and I will sanctify him before the people; for unto him have I given *the keys of this kingdom and ministry.* Even so. Amen. (Doctrine and Covenants 115:19)

LATTER-DAY MISSIONARIES

Behold, I sent you out to testify and warn the people, and it becometh every man who hath been warned to warn his neighbor.

Therefore, they are left without excuse, and their sins are upon their own heads.

He that seeketh me early shall find me, and shall not be forsaken.

Therefore, tarry ye, and labor diligently, that you may be *perfected in your ministry* to go forth among the Gentiles for the last time, as many as the mouth of the Lord shall name, to bind up the law and seal up the testimony, and to prepare the saints for the hour of judgment which is to come. (Doctrine and Covenants 88:81–84)

LATTER-DAY DISCIPLES

Behold, this is the tithing and the sacrifice which I, the Lord, require at their hands, that there may be a house built unto me for the salvation of Zion—

For a place of thanksgiving for all saints, and for a place of instruction for all those who are called to *the work of the ministry* in all their several callings and offices;

That they may be perfected in *the understanding of their ministry,* in theory, in principle, and in doctrine, in all things pertaining to the kingdom of God on the earth, the keys of which kingdom have been conferred upon you. (Doctrine and Covenants 97:12–14)

Nevertheless, ye shall not cast him out of your synagogues, or your places of worship, for *unto such shall ye continue to minister;* for ye know not but what they will return and repent, and come unto me with full purpose of heart, and I shall heal them; and ye shall be the means of bringing salvation unto them. (3 Nephi 18:32)

AN INSTITUTION TO BLESS INDIVIDUALS

One of the overarching purposes of the restored Church as an institution is to facilitate ministering to individuals and families *one by one.*

"The Church of Jesus Christ of Latter-day Saints was organized by God to assist in His work to bring to pass the salvation and exaltation of His children. The Church invites *all* to 'come unto Christ, and be perfected in him' (Moroni 10:32; see also D&C 20:59). The invitation to come unto Christ pertains to *all* who have lived, or will ever live, on the earth.

"When *individuals* receive the ordinances of baptism and confirmation, they become members of the Church. The Church supports them and their families by serving as 'a refuge from the storm' of worldly influences and wickedness (D&C 115:6). The Church provides opportunities for service, blessing, and personal growth. The programs and activities of the Church support and strengthen *individuals and families.*

"In fulfilling its purpose to help *individuals and families* qualify for exaltation, the Church focuses on divinely appointed responsibilities. These include helping members live the gospel of Jesus Christ, gathering Israel through missionary work, caring for the poor and needy, and enabling the salvation of the dead by building temples and performing vicarious ordinances" (*Handbook 2: Administering the Church,* 2.2).

The Church is the authorized repository and safeguard for the essential doctrine, priesthood authority and keys, and holy ordinances and covenants that enable the sons and daughters of God to progress according to the Father's eternal plan of happiness. Please note how the language in *Handbook 2: Administering the Church* connects the purposes and activities of the Church as an organization to the spiritual development and growth of *individuals and families.*

Elder D. Todd Christofferson addressed the question of "Why the Church" and explained the spiritually essential role of the restored Church of Jesus Christ as an institution.

"The Church is the creation of Him in whom our spirituality is centered—Jesus Christ. It is worth pausing to consider why He chooses to use a church, His Church, The Church of Jesus Christ of Latter-day Saints, to carry out His and His Father's work 'to bring to pass the immortality and eternal life of man' [Moses 1:39].

"Beginning with Adam, the gospel of Jesus Christ was preached, and the essential ordinances of salvation, such as baptism, were administered through a family-based priesthood order. As societies grew more complex than simply extended families, God also called other prophets, messengers, and teachers. In Moses's time, we read of a more formal structure, including elders, priests, and judges. In Book of Mormon history, Alma established a church with priests and teachers.

"Then, in the meridian of time, Jesus organized His work in such a way that the gospel could be established simultaneously in multiple nations and among diverse peoples. That organization, the Church of Jesus Christ, was founded on 'apostles and prophets, Jesus Christ himself being the chief corner stone' [Ephesians 2:20]. It included additional officers, such as seventies, elders, bishops, priests, teachers, and deacons. Jesus similarly established the Church in the Western Hemisphere after His Resurrection.

"Following the apostasy and disintegration of the Church He had organized while on the earth, the Lord reestablished the Church of Jesus Christ once again through the Prophet Joseph Smith. The ancient purpose remains: that is, to preach the good news of the gospel of Jesus Christ and administer the ordinances of salvation—in other words, to bring people to Christ. And now, through the instrumentality of this restored Church, the promise of redemption is placed within reach even of the spirits of the dead who in their mortal lifetime knew little or nothing of the Savior's grace.

"How does His Church accomplish the Lord's purposes? It is important to recognize that God's ultimate purpose is our progress. His desire is that we continue 'from grace to grace, until [we receive] a fulness' of all He can give [Doctrine and Covenants 93:13]. That requires more than simply being nice or feeling spiritual. It requires faith in Jesus Christ, repentance, baptism of water and of the Spirit, and enduring in faith to the end. One cannot fully achieve this in isolation, so a major reason the Lord has a church is to create a community of Saints that will sustain one another in the 'strait and narrow path which leads to eternal life' [2 Nephi 31:18]" ("Why the Church," *Ensign,* November 2015).

The Church of Jesus Christ as an *institution* is one of the principal tools used by the Savior to facilitate divinely orchestrated opportunities for His disciples to minister to *individuals and families one by one.* Unfortunately, however, the sacred work of the ministry in the Church and by members can be obscured by a phenomenon known as means vs. ends confusion.

The phrase *a means to an end* differentiates between an end goal and the means or methods and actions used to achieve that goal. For example, home and visiting teaching statistics (the means) can be used to assess partially the effectiveness of men and women in fulfilling their responsibility to watch over, be with, and spiritually strengthen (the ends) those whom they serve. But an inordinate and inappropriate focus on simply improving statistical performance can supplant the intended purpose of these inspired programs. Statistics may replace service as a consequence of means vs. ends confusion.

Elder Jeffrey R. Holland implored holders of the priesthood to focus upon the proper "ends"—*individuals and families*—in fulfilling their home teaching responsibilities. "The appeal I am making . . . is for you to lift your vision of home teaching. Please, in newer, better ways see yourselves as emissaries of the Lord to His children. That means leaving behind the tradition of a frantic, law of Moses–like, end-of-the-month calendar in which you rush to give a scripted message from the Church magazines that the family has already read. We would hope, rather, that you will establish an era of genuine, gospel-oriented concern for the members, watching over and caring for each other, addressing spiritual and temporal needs in any way that helps. . . . What matters is that you love your people and are fulfilling the commandment 'to watch over the church always' [Doctrine and Covenants 20:54]" ("Emissaries to the Church," *Ensign,* November 2016).

All of us at some time have said or heard the phrase, "Next Sunday I am teaching a lesson about repentance"—or about some other gospel principle or topic. However, we do not teach lessons; we teach people. Excessively emphasizing lesson content and delivery can lead to deemphasizing the needs of individuals in a class and to altogether missing divinely orchestrated opportunities to lift, strengthen, and clarify *one by one.* Thirty individuals do not constitute a class; rather, a class is comprised of thirty individual *ones.*

Elder Dallin H. Oaks described the role of teaching in the home and at Church: "A gospel teacher, like the Master we serve, will concentrate entirely on those being taught. His or her total concentration will be on the needs of the sheep—the good of the students. A gospel teacher does not focus on himself or herself. One who understands that principle will not look upon his or her calling as 'giving or presenting a lesson,' because that definition views teaching from the standpoint of the teacher, not the student. Focusing on the needs of the students, a gospel teacher will never obscure their view of the Master by standing in the way or by shadowing the lesson with self-promotion or self-interest" ("Gospel Teaching," *Ensign,* November 1999).

One of the most disconcerting examples of means vs. ends confusion in the Church occurs between programs and people. Church programs are intended to help members learn and live in accordance with gospel principles. But managing programs can take priority over ministering to people, and program performance can overshadow the important work of helping *individuals* to grow and develop.

The following statement from *Handbook 2: Administering the Church* clearly articulates the proper means vs. ends relationship between Church programs and people.

"In the teachings and practices of the restored gospel, the family and the Church help and strengthen each other. To qualify for the blessings of eternal life, families need to learn the doctrines and receive the priesthood ordinances that are available only through the Church. To be a strong and vital organization, the Church needs righteous families.

"God has revealed a pattern of spiritual progress for *individuals and families* through ordinances, teaching, programs, and activities that are *home centered and Church supported. Church organizations and programs exist to bless individuals and families and are not ends in themselves.* Priesthood and auxiliary leaders and teachers seek to assist parents, not to supersede or replace them.

"Priesthood and auxiliary leaders must endeavor to strengthen the sacredness of the home by ensuring that all Church activities support the lives of *individuals and families.* Church leaders need to be careful not to overwhelm families with too many Church responsibilities. Parents and Church leaders work together to help *individuals and families* return to our Father in Heaven by following Jesus Christ" (*Handbook 2: Administering the Church,* 1.4).

Elder M. Russell Ballard counseled all Church members: "Brothers and sisters, may we focus on the simple ways we can serve in the kingdom of God, always striving to change lives, including our own. What is most important in our Church responsibilities is not the statistics that are reported or the meetings that are held but whether or not individual people—ministered to one at a time just as the Savior did—have been lifted and encouraged and ultimately changed. Our task is to help others find the peace and the joy that only the gospel can give them" ("O Be Wise," *Ensign,* November 2006).

THE LORD'S PATTERN OF ONE BY ONE IN HIS RESTORED CHURCH

The restored Church provides the structure and means for teaching the gospel of Jesus Christ to all of God's children and the priesthood authority to administer the ordinances of salvation and exaltation to all who are worthy and willing to accept them. All of the divinely appointed responsibilities that constitute the very purpose of the Lord's restored Church are focused upon *individuals and families*: (1) helping members live the gospel of Jesus Christ, (2) gathering Israel through missionary work, (3) caring for the poor and needy, and (4) enabling the salvation of the dead by building temples and performing vicarious ordinances.

President Howard W. Hunter noted: "I have always been impressed that the Lord deals with us personally, individually. We do many things in groups in the Church, . . . but . . . the most important things are done *individually*. We bless babies *one at a time,* even if they are twins or triplets. We baptize and confirm children *one at a time.* We take the sacrament, are ordained to the priesthood, or move through the ordinances of the temple as *individuals*—as *one person* developing a [personal] relationship with our Father in Heaven. . . . *Heaven's emphasis is on each individual, on every single person*" ("Eternal Investments," address to CES religious educators, February 10, 1989).

I invite you to now consider four illustrative aspects of the gospel and the Savior's restored Church that exemplify the principle of *one by one.* Many additional teachings and practices also demonstrate this principle; these four are selected as representative examples.

ORDINANCES

Holy ordinances are central in the Savior's gospel and in the process of coming unto Him and seeking spiritual rebirth. Ordinances such as baptism, confirmation, and the sacrament are sacred acts that have spiritual purpose and eternal significance and are related to God's laws and statutes. The symbolism of ordinances helps the participants remember the Father's love, the Son's Atonement, and the Holy Ghost's influence.

"Ordinances have always been part of the gospel of Jesus Christ. Baptism, for example, was established in the days of Adam and Eve and is practiced in the Lord's Church today. Church members are commanded to gather together often to partake of the sacrament to remember the Savior always and to renew the covenants and blessings of baptism (see Moroni 6:6; D&C 59:8–9).

"Some ordinances are required for exaltation in the celestial kingdom for all accountable persons. These ordinances include baptism, confirmation, Melchizedek Priesthood ordination (for men), the temple endowment, and temple sealing. Living members of the Church receive these saving and exalting ordinances themselves. Deceased persons may receive them vicariously. Vicarious ordinances become effective only when the deceased persons for whom the ordinances were performed accept them in the spirit world and honor the related covenants" (*Handbook 2: Administering the Church,* 2.1.2).

All saving ordinances and the ordinance of the sacrament must be authorized by one who holds the requisite priesthood keys.

The ordinances of salvation and exaltation administered in the Lord's restored Church are far more than rituals or symbolic performances. Rather, they constitute authorized channels through which the blessings and powers of heaven can flow into our individual lives.

Priesthood ordinances are the pathway to the power of godliness: "And this greater priesthood administereth the gospel and holdeth the key of the mysteries of the kingdom, even the key of the knowledge of God. Therefore, in the ordinances thereof, the power of godliness is manifest. And without the ordinances thereof, and the authority of the priesthood, the power of godliness is not manifest unto men in the flesh" (Doctrine and Covenants 84:19–21).

Priesthood ordinances are administered using the Lord's

pattern of *one by one*. The resurrected Savior Himself taught that holy ordinances are to be performed individually. For example, He detailed the procedure for performing the ordinance of baptism:

> Verily I say unto you, that whoso repenteth of his sins through your words, and desireth to be baptized in my name, on this wise shall ye baptize them—Behold, ye shall go down and stand in the water, and in my name shall ye baptize them.
>
> And now behold, these are the words which ye shall say, calling them by name, saying:
>
> Having authority given me of Jesus Christ, I baptize you in the name of the Father, and of the Son, and of the Holy Ghost. Amen.
>
> And then shall ye immerse them in the water, and come forth again out of the water. (3 Nephi 11:23–26)

Please note that each person was to be specifically called by name and then immersed *individually* in the water by the one performing the ordinance.

Nephi baptized the disciples in the manner prescribed—*one by one*. The record states, "And it came to pass that Nephi went down into the water and was baptized. And he came up out of the water and began to baptize. And he baptized all those whom Jesus had chosen" (3 Nephi 19:11–12).

The Book of Mormon confirms that those baptized were ministered to as *individuals.*

> And it came to pass when they were all baptized and had come up out of the water, the Holy Ghost did fall upon them, and they were filled with the Holy Ghost and with fire.
>
> And behold, they were encircled about as if it were by fire; and it came down from heaven, and the multitude did witness it, and did bear record; and angels did come down out of heaven and did minister unto them.
>
> And it came to pass that while the angels were ministering unto the disciples, behold, Jesus came and stood in the midst and ministered unto them. (3 Nephi 19:13–15)

The ordinances of baptism by immersion for the remission of sins, the laying on of the hands for the gift of the Holy Ghost, and confirmation as a member of The Church of Jesus Christ of Latter-day Saints all are administered and received *one by one.*

The ordinance of the sacrament is a holy and repeated invitation to repent sincerely and to be renewed spiritually. Priesthood holders offer the bread and the water to the members of the

Church *one by one*. Members of the Church receive the sacramental emblems *one by one*.

The act of partaking of the sacrament, in and of itself, does not remit sins. But as we prepare conscientiously and participate in this holy ordinance with a broken heart and a contrite spirit, then the promise is that we may always have the Spirit of the Lord to be with us. And by the sanctifying power of the Holy Ghost as our constant companion, we can always retain a remission of our sins.

We truly are blessed each week by the opportunity to evaluate our lives through the ordinance of the sacrament, to renew our covenants, and to receive this covenant promise.

Ordinances are administered and received *one by one*— because the worth of souls is great in the sight of God.

COVENANTS

"And also my soul delighteth in the covenants of the Lord which he hath made to our fathers; yea, my soul delighteth in his grace, and in his justice, and power, and mercy in the great and eternal plan of deliverance from death" (2 Nephi 11:5).

The Lord's instruction about sacred covenants to Emma Smith in 1830 applies equally to each of us today: "Wherefore, lift up thy heart and rejoice, and cleave unto the covenants which thou hast made" (Doctrine and Covenants 25:13).

"All the ordinances necessary for salvation and exaltation are accompanied by covenants with God. A covenant is a sacred and enduring promise between God and His children. God gives the conditions for the covenant, and His children agree to comply with those conditions. God promises blessings that are conditional on the person faithfully fulfilling the covenant.

"As Church members honor and keep their covenants, they are greatly blessed in mortality and become eligible for exaltation (see Exodus 19:3–5; Judges 2:1; 3 Nephi 20:25–27; Moroni 10:33; D&C 42:78; 97:8).

"To prepare an *individual* for participation in an ordinance, parents, other family members, priesthood and auxiliary leaders, and teachers ensure that the person understands the covenants he or she will make (see Mosiah 18:8–11). After the ordinance, they help him or her keep those covenants (see Mosiah 18:23–26)" (*Handbook 2: Administering the Church,* 2.1.3).

Because Heavenly Father and His Beloved Son know us as individuals, covenants are received according to the spiritual pattern of *one by one.* Elder Jeffrey R. Holland emphasized the individual nature of covenants.

"A covenant is a binding spiritual contract, a solemn promise to God our Father that we will live and think and act in a certain way—the way of His Son, the Lord Jesus Christ. In return, the Father, Son, and Holy Ghost promise us the full splendor of eternal life.

"It is interesting to me that covenants are made personally, *individually.* There is a covenant at the time of baptism and confirmation, which starts us on the way to eternal life. Those ordinances are performed for individual persons, *one by one,* no matter how many must ultimately receive them.

"There is a covenant at the time men receive the priesthood. That conferral is always given to *one individual* at a time.

"The highest covenants we can make are in the temple. That is where we make our most solemn promises to our Father in Heaven and where He opens to us more fully the real meaning of His promises to us. Once again, these are *individual* experiences, even as we go to the temple to be sealed to other individuals.

"That's how the kingdom of God is built—*one person* at a time, one covenant at a time, all roads in our mortal journey leading to the ultimate covenants of the holy temple" ("Keeping Covenants: A Message for Those Who Will Serve a Mission," *New Era,* January 2012).

The Savior said: "Come unto me, all ye that labour and are heavy laden, and I will give you rest.

"Take my yoke upon you, and learn of me; for I am meek and lowly in heart: and ye shall find rest unto your souls.

"For my yoke is easy, and my burden is light" (Matthew 11:28–30).

A yoke is a wooden beam, normally used between a pair of oxen or other animals that enables them to pull together on a load. A yoke places animals side by side so they can move together in order to accomplish a task.

Consider the Lord's uniquely individual invitation to "take my yoke upon you." Making and keeping sacred covenants yokes us to and with the Lord Jesus Christ. In essence, the Savior is beckoning us to rely upon and pull together with Him, even though our best efforts are not equal to and cannot be compared with His. As we trust in and pull our load with Him during the journey of mortality, truly His yoke is easy, and His burden is light.

Covenants are administered and received *one by one*—because the worth of souls is great in the sight of God.

RESCUE WORK

The work of rescuing spiritually lost souls is best accomplished using the Lord's pattern of *one by one*.

"For Latter-day Saints, the need to rescue our brothers and sisters who have, for one reason or another, strayed from the path of Church activity is of eternal significance. . . .

"Consider the lost among the aged, the widowed, and the sick. All too often they are found in the parched and desolate wilderness of isolation called loneliness. When youth departs, when health declines, when vigor wanes, when the light of hope flickers ever so dimly, they can be succored and sustained by the hand that helps and the heart that knows compassion.

"There are, of course, others who need rescue. Some struggle with sin while others wander in fear or apathy or ignorance. For whatever reason, they have isolated themselves from activity in the

Church. And they will almost certainly remain lost unless there awakens in us—the active members of the Church—a desire to rescue and to save. . . .

"During the Master's ministry, He called fishermen at Galilee to leave their nets and follow Him, declaring, 'I will make you fishers of men' [Matthew 4:19]. May we join the ranks of the fishers of men and women, that we might provide whatever help we can.

"Ours is the duty to reach out to rescue those who have left the safety of activity, that such might be brought to the table of the Lord to feast on His word, to enjoy the companionship of His Spirit, and to be 'no more strangers and foreigners, but fellowcitizens with the saints, and of the household of God' [Ephesians 2:19].

". . . Two fundamental reasons largely account for a return to activity and for changes of attitudes, habits, and actions. First, individuals return because someone has shown them their eternal possibilities and has helped them decide to achieve them. The less active can't long rest content with mediocrity once they see that excellence is within their reach.

"Second, others return because loved ones or 'fellowcitizens with the saints' have followed the admonition of the Savior, have loved their neighbors as themselves, and have helped others to bring their dreams to fulfillment and their ambitions to realization.

"The catalyst in this process has been—and will continue to be—the principle of love. . . .

"May we reach out to rescue the lost who surround us: the aged, the widowed, the sick, those with disabilities, the less active, and those who are not keeping the commandments. May we extend to them the hand that helps and the heart that knows compassion. By doing so, we will bring joy into their hearts, and we will experience the rich satisfaction that comes to us when we help another along the pathway to eternal life" (Thomas S. Monson, "Our Responsibility to Rescue," *Ensign,* October 2013).

Please consider the potential impact across many generations of just *one* soul who returns to the path of devoted gospel living and Church activity. Several years ago, Elder L. Tom Perry described in a BYU devotional message the legacy of Gustavus Adolphus Perry, the first member of the Perry family to join The Church of Jesus Christ of Latter-day Saints. In 1997, as the Perry family prepared to celebrate the 200th birthday of Gustavus Perry, Elder Perry's brother conducted extensive research and identified as many of the descendants of Gustavus and his wife, Eunice, as he could. In your mind, please try to guess the number of descendants Elder Perry's brother found.

The answer—more than 10,000 family members comprised the posterity of this faithful man and woman.

Elder Perry explained: "The number overwhelmed me. I could not believe that there could be more than 10,000 descendants of Gustavus Adolphus Perry. In seven to eight generations, his family had sufficient numbers to organize three stakes of the Church" ("The Value of a Good Name," BYU Devotional, February 11, 1997).

As this story about Elder Perry's family illustrates, each and every *one* is an important link in a chain of the generations. *One-by-one* addition and multiplication over decades can influence innumerable souls for righteousness. Perhaps this celestial calculus undergirds the profound admonition from the Savior presented at the beginning of this chapter:

"Nevertheless, ye shall not cast him out of your synagogues, or your places of worship, for *unto such shall ye continue to minister;* for ye know not but what they will return and repent, and come unto me with full purpose of heart, and I shall heal them; and ye shall be the means of bringing salvation unto them" (3 Nephi 18:32).

"This work of reactivation often involves group study and socials, but, essentially, it is done *a soul at a time,* quietly and with dignity. It is done less 'by the numbers' and more 'by the Spirit.' It is less technique than genuine caring, more extending a helping hand than writing new handbooks" (Neal A. Maxwell, "'A Brother Offended,'" *Ensign,* May 1982).

Rescue work is best accomplished *one by one*—because the worth of souls is great in the sight of God.

CHURCH COUNCILS

"The Lord's Church is governed through councils at the general, area, stake, and ward levels. These councils are fundamental to the order of the Church.

"Under the keys of priesthood leadership at each level, leaders counsel together for the benefit of *individuals and families.* Council members also plan the work of the Church pertaining to their assignments. Effective councils invite full expression from council members and unify their efforts in responding to *individual, family, and organizational needs*" (*Handbook 2: Administering the Church,* 4.1).

The ultimate purpose of Church councils is to learn about and apply effectively the Lord's pattern of ministering *one by one.* Because the work of the ministry is focused principally upon people and not programs, councils should facilitate the revelatory process for addressing the needs and concerns of *individuals and families*—not just organizational issues. Councils are not simply business meetings conducted to direct and coordinate activities; rather, they should be revelatory experiences intended to bless and strengthen people.

Elder M. Russell Ballard has observed: "Sometimes we get so focused on bringing people to the meetinghouse that we forget we are supposed to be bringing them to Christ. Too often, our council meetings reflect that lack of focus. We find ourselves spending all of our precious time during council meetings coordinating events and correlating schedules. Instead of doing the Lord's business—which almost always has to do with touching the lives of *individuals and families*—we allow ourselves to get bogged down in administrative busyness. Reports are submitted and assignments are made and the meeting is considered a success, even though there has been no serious discussion of how to move the organization forward in proclaiming the gospel, perfecting the Saints, and redeeming the dead—each of which involves touching and influencing people.

"If your calling has become simply a long list of things that need to be done—activities that need to be planned, lessons that need to be prepared, assignments that need to be filled, meetings that need to be held—it can be daunting. It is only when we get beyond the administrative details of our callings and focus our attentions on the principles of ministering to God's children and bringing the blessings of the gospel into their lives that our Church offices take on their full meaning, and we experience the fulfilling joy and satisfaction to be found in rendering significant service in the kingdom.

"By focusing attention on . . . issues that stem directly from our efforts to accomplish the mission of the Church, presiding councils shift their vision from administration to ministration, and the council members experience the joy that comes from making a meaningful difference in people's lives" (*Counseling with Our Councils* [1997], 71–73).

Church councils are intended to focus upon and facilitate ministering to individuals and families *one by one*—because the worth of souls is great in the sight of God.

ONE BY ONE—INDIVIDUALLY AND TOGETHER

Even though ordinances and covenants are administered and received by individuals *one by one,* there is great purpose and power in gathering as disciples to remember and renew our sacred commitments. What we receive individually can be enlarged and enriched as we study and serve together.

> Yea, even he commanded them that they should preach nothing save it were repentance and faith on the Lord, who had redeemed his people.
>
> And he commanded them that there should be no contention one with another, but that they should look forward with one eye, having one faith and one baptism, *having their hearts knit together in unity and in love one towards another.*
>
> And thus he commanded them to preach. And thus they became the children of God. (Mosiah 18:20–22)

President Gordon B. Hinckley encouraged faithful members of the Church all around the world: "I would hope, I would pray,

that each of us . . . would resolve to seek those who need help
. . . and lift them in the spirit of love into the embrace of the
Church, where strong hands and loving hearts will warm them,
comfort them, sustain them, and put them on the way of happy
and productive lives" (" 'Reach with a Rescuing Hand,' " *Ensign,*
November 1996).

On the day he was sustained as the President of The Church
of Jesus Christ of Latter-day Saints, President Hinckley described
the importance of every member and every service performed in
the Church.

"This church does not belong to its President. Its head is the
Lord Jesus Christ, whose name each of us has taken upon ourselves. We are all in this great endeavor together. We are here to
assist our Father in His work and His glory, 'to bring to pass the
immortality and eternal life of man' (Moses 1:39). *Your obligation
is as serious in your sphere of responsibility as is my obligation in my
sphere. No calling in this church is small or of little consequence. All
of us in the pursuit of our duty touch the lives of others. . . .*

"All of us in this great cause are of one mind, of one belief, of
one faith.

"*You have as great an opportunity for satisfaction in the performance of your duty as I do in mine.* The progress of this work will
be determined by our joint efforts. Whatever your calling, it is as
fraught with the same kind of opportunity to accomplish good
as is mine. *What is really important is that this is the work of the*

Master. Our work is to go about doing good as did He" ("This Is the Work of the Master," *Ensign,* May 1995).

How can the service of a ward Primary teacher or a youth leader possibly be as important as the work of the President of the Lord's restored Church? Perhaps, in part, President Hinckley was emphasizing the importance of the Lord's pattern of ministering *one by one*. The work of the Master always focuses upon *individuals and families*. Whether we serve as a home or visiting teacher, as a General Authority, as an auxiliary leader, or as a Sunday School teacher, our opportunities to minister to individuals are great and significant. The President of the Church and a home or visiting teacher perform their respective duties in different locations and times—but the essence of the work is precisely the same.

The Lord's pattern of ministering *one by one* is central and pervasive in His restored Church—because the worth of souls is great in the sight of God.

SUMMARY

The Church of Jesus Christ of Latter-day Saints is a workshop in which we gain experience as we practice on each other in the ongoing process of perfecting the Saints. Elder Neal A. Maxwell insightfully explained that in this latter-day learning laboratory known as the restored Church, the members constitute the "clinical material" that is essential for growth and development (see "Jesus, the Perfect Mentor," *Ensign,* February 2001).

A visiting teacher learns her duty as she serves and loves her Relief Society sisters.

An inexperienced teacher learns valuable lessons as he teaches both supportive and inattentive learners and thereby becomes a more effective teacher.

A new bishop learns how to be a bishop through inspiration and by working with ward members who wholeheartedly sustain him, even while recognizing his human frailties.

And in every ordinance and covenant, in every lesson and class, in every act of service by a home or visiting teacher, in every effort to rescue a lost soul, and in every council meeting that focuses upon the needs of *individuals and families*, we learn of Him.

"Learn of me, and listen to my words; walk in the meekness of my Spirit, and you shall have peace in me.

"I am Jesus Christ; I came by the will of the Father, and I do his will" (Doctrine and Covenants 19:23–24).

As we learn, listen, and walk in His ways, we come to understand that each of us—*one by one*—has an individual responsibility to learn and live the principles of the restored gospel and exercise faith in the Lord Jesus Christ.

Each of us—*one by one*—has an individual responsibility to repent.

The ordinance of baptism by immersion for the remission of sins is administered and received *one by one*.

The ordinance of confirmation and the bestowal of the gift of the Holy Ghost is administered *one by one.*

Conferral of priesthood authority and ordination to priesthood offices is performed *one by one.*

In the ordinance of the sacrament, the emblems of the Savior's body and blood, the bread and water, are given to the members of a congregation and received *one by one.*

Calls to serve as full-time missionaries are extended and assignments to labor in specific locations are made *one by one.*

Missionaries seek out and teach investigators *one by one.*

Patriarchal blessings are given *one by one.*

The setting apart of teachers and officers in all Church organizations and programs is done *one by one.*

Thus, in the Savior's restored Church upon the earth, His pattern of ministering *one by one* is evident in all things that are spiritually and eternally essential.

> *It may not be on the mountain height*
> *Or over the stormy sea,*
> *It may not be at the battle's front*
> *My Lord will have need of me.*
> *But if, by a still, small voice he calls*
> *To paths that I do not know,*
> *I'll answer, dear Lord, with my hand in thine:*
> *I'll go where you want me to go.*

Perhaps today there are loving words
Which Jesus would have me speak;
There may be now in the paths of sin
Some wand'rer whom I should seek.
O Savior, if thou wilt be my guide,
Tho dark and rugged the way,
My voice shall echo the message sweet:
I'll say what you want me to say.

There's surely somewhere a lowly place
In earth's harvest fields so wide
Where I may labor through life's short day
For Jesus, the Crucified.
So trusting my all to thy tender care,
And knowing thou lovest me,
I'll do thy will with a heart sincere:
I'll be what you want me to be.
(Hymns *[1985]*, no. 270)

Questions to Consider

1. What can and should I do to better understand the relationship between "means" and "ends" in the work of the ministry?

2. How does increasing my understanding about the work of the ministry affect my motives, my heart, and my behavior?

3. What can and should I do in my life to focus more effectively

upon individuals and families, not just programs and activities, and to become more Christlike in my personal ministry?

My Own Questions to Consider

1. _____

_____

2. _____

_____

3. _____

_____

Scriptures Related to What I Am Learning

_____

_____

_____

CHAPTER 5

ONE BY ONE AND THE TENDER MERCIES OF THE LORD

While fulfilling an assignment, I met and became acquainted with a man who recently had lost his wife. Her death was unexpected and sudden. His heart was aching, but his knowledge of the Father's plan of salvation and his deep faith in the Lord Jesus Christ provided comfort and peace as he pressed forward during a most difficult time in his life.

As I talked with this good man, he expressed concern about his missionary son. The young elder, who had been serving valiantly in his assigned field of labor for almost a year, was especially close to his mother. The missionary had elected to remain in the mission field and did not attend her funeral. The elder had talked with his father on several occasions and reported that he was doing well, even though the loss of his mother was a hard thing for him. But the father naturally worried that her passing might be spiritually unsettling to his son and divert his attention from the work he had been called to do.

I asked this man where his son was serving. We both were delighted to learn that I was scheduled to meet with the missionaries in his son's mission in two weeks. I shook the man's hand, hugged him, and promised that I would convey his handshake and hug to his missionary. I also indicated that I would spend some time and talk with his son during my visit. And I pledged to call the father and update him about his son after I returned home from my assignment.

I personally believe the opportunity to talk with this missionary could not have come at a better time. The young elder and I considered together the purposes of death in the Father's plan, the Resurrection made possible through the Savior's infinite and eternal atoning sacrifice, the importance of discerning the Lord's will and timing in our lives, and the well-being of this elder's family back home. Most important, the handshake and hug I conveyed from his father were meaningful to this young servant of the Lord. My conversation with his father when I returned home from my assignment was also a memorable experience for me.

Was it merely a coincidence that I encountered this man on my assignment? Was it just a random event that I was scheduled to meet with all the missionaries in his son's mission in just two weeks? Or was this episode divinely orchestrated by a loving Lord who knew and responded to the concerns of a devoted father—a *one?* I believe that in the work of the Lord there is no such thing as a coincidence. The worth of souls is great in the sight of God.

THE TENDER MERCIES OF THE LORD

"But behold, I, Nephi, will show unto you that the tender mercies of the Lord are over all those whom he hath chosen, because of their faith, to make them mighty even unto the power of deliverance" (1 Nephi 1:20).

The Lord's tender mercies are the very personal and individualized blessings, strength, protection, assurances, guidance, lovingkindnesses, consolation, support, and spiritual gifts that we receive from and because of and through the Lord Jesus Christ. Truly, the Lord suits "his mercies according to the conditions of the children of men" (D&C 46:15).

I testify that the tender mercies of the Lord are real and that they do not occur randomly or merely by coincidence. Often, the Lord's timing of His tender mercies helps us to both discern and acknowledge them.

The word *chosen* in 1 Nephi 1:20 is central to understanding the concept of the Lord's tender mercies. The dictionary indicates that *chosen* suggests one who is selected, taken by preference, or picked out. The word also can be used to refer to the elect or chosen of God (see *Oxford English Dictionary Online,* second ed. [1989], "Chosen").

Some individuals may discount or dismiss in their personal lives the availability of the tender mercies of the Lord, believing that "I certainly am not one who has been or ever will be chosen." We may falsely think that such blessings and gifts are reserved for other people who appear to be more righteous or who serve in more visible Church callings. I testify that the tender mercies of the Lord are available to all of us and that the Redeemer of Israel is eager to bestow such gifts upon us. The worth of souls is great in the sight of God.

To be or to become chosen is not an exclusive status conferred upon us. Rather, you and I ultimately determine if we are chosen. Please note the use of the word *chosen* in the following verses from the Doctrine and Covenants.

> But behold, verily I say unto you, that there are many who have been ordained among you, whom I have called but few of them are *chosen.*
>
> They who are not *chosen* have sinned a very grievous sin, in that they are walking in darkness at noonday. (Doctrine and Covenants 95:5–6)
>
> Behold, there are many called, but few are *chosen.* And why are they not *chosen?*

> Because their hearts are set so much upon the
> things of this world, and aspire to the honors of men.
> (Doctrine and Covenants 121:34–35)

I believe the implication of these verses is quite straightforward. God does not have a list of favorites to which we must hope our names will someday be added. He does not limit "the chosen" to a restricted few. Rather, it is *our* hearts and *our* aspirations and *our* obedience that definitively determine whether we are counted among God's chosen.

The fundamental purposes for the gift of moral agency are to love one another and to choose God (see Moses 7:32–33). Thus, we become God's chosen and invite His tender mercies as we use our agency to choose Him.

TENDER MERCIES AND THE SPIRITUAL PATTERN OF MINISTERING ONE BY ONE

Tender mercies are individualized and timely blessings that are manifested in a multitude of ways. Sometimes a tender mercy is delivered directly from the Lord by the power of the Holy Ghost. I now repeat from one of my general conference messages an example of how a tender mercy was conveyed to a widow directly from heaven (see "The Tender Mercies of the Lord," *Ensign*, May 2005).

In a Saturday evening session of stake conference, the tender mercies of the Lord were evident in the touching testimony of a young wife and mother of four whose husband was slain in Iraq in December of 2003. This stalwart sister recounted how, after being notified of her husband's death, she received his Christmas card and message. In the midst of the abrupt reality of a dramatically altered life came to this good sister a timely and tender reminder that indeed families can be together forever. With permission, I quote from that Christmas card:

"To the best family in the world! Have a great time together and remember the true meaning of Christmas! The Lord has made it possible for us to be together forever. So even when we are apart, we will still be together as a family.

"God bless and keep y'all safe and grant this Christmas to be our gift of love from us to Him above!!!

"All my love, Daddy and your loving husband!"

Clearly, the husband's reference to being apart in his Christmas greeting referred to the separation caused by his military assignment. But to this sister, as a voice from the dust from a departed eternal companion and father, came a most needed spiritual reassurance and witness. The Lord's tender mercies do not occur randomly or merely by coincidence. Faithfulness, obedience, and humility invite tender mercies into our lives, and it is often the Lord's timing that enables us to recognize and treasure these important blessings.

Was it merely a coincidence that this letter contained the message it did and arrived when it did? Or was this episode divinely orchestrated by a loving Lord who knew and responded to the concerns of a grieving widow—a *one?* I believe that in the work of the Lord there is no such thing as a coincidence. And this tender mercy was delivered directly from heaven—because the worth of souls is great in the sight of God.

Tender mercies also are frequently delivered *one by one* through the instrumentality of another person. As President Spencer W. Kimball taught, "God does notice us, and he watches over us. But it is usually through another person that he meets our needs. Therefore, it is vital that we serve each other" (*Teachings of Presidents of the Church: Spencer W. Kimball* [2006], 82). As we learn in the hymn "Each Life That Touches Ours for Good":

> *Each life that touches ours for good*
> *Reflects thine own great mercy, Lord;*
> *Thou sendest blessings from above*
> *Thru words and deeds of those who love.*

> *What greater gift dost thou bestow,*
> *What greater goodness can we know*
> *Than Christlike friends, whose gentle ways*
> *Strengthen our faith, enrich our days.*
> (Hymns *[1985], no. 293*)

It is important to remember that each member of the Lord's restored Church has a personal and *one-by-one* ministry to perform with family members, friends, and other Latter-day Saints. In this individualized work of the ministry, the Savior frequently relies upon us to deliver His tender mercies. Sometimes we may be aware of the role we are performing in accomplishing God's purposes; many times—and perhaps even most—we are not.

Before attending her sacrament meetings, my wife, Susan, frequently prays for the spiritual eyes to see those who have a need. Often as she observes the brothers and sisters and children in the congregation, she will feel a spiritual nudge to visit with or make a phone call to a particular person. And when Susan receives such an impression, she promptly responds and obeys. It often is the case that as soon as the "amen" is spoken in the benediction, she will talk with a teenager or hug a sister or, upon returning home, immediately pick up the phone and make a call. As long as I have known Susan, people have marveled at her capacity to discern and respond to individual needs. Often they will ask her, "How did you know?" In her personal ministry, Susan has been a tool in the hands of the Lord to deliver tender mercies *one by one* to many people—because the worth of souls is great in the sight of God.

The selected episodes that follow provide additional examples of how the tender mercies of the Lord are often delivered *one by one* through the instrumentality of other people. These illustrations are not presented in a particular order and are only a sample of the many ways tender mercies can be conveyed.

LEAVING A PRIESTHOOD LEADERSHIP MEETING

Many years ago, while serving as a stake president, I was scheduled to preside at and participate in a stake priesthood leadership meeting. The gathering was to be held in our stake center located approximately 65 miles from our home. The drive to the stake center typically required from 70 to 85 minutes, depending upon weather and road conditions.

The leadership session was to begin at 4:30 p.m. Sitting on the stand a few minutes before the starting time, I turned to one of my counselors and whispered, "If I need to leave early today, can you cover for me?" He asked if something was wrong or if I was getting sick. I replied that everything was fine; I simply thought it might be necessary for me to leave the meeting. He responded, with a quizzical look on his face, "Sure, we can handle it if you need to take off."

I motioned to the stake executive secretary and asked him to invite a brother in the congregation who was serving as an elders quorum president to meet me in my office immediately. I left the stand, walked to the stake president's office, and waited for the brother to arrive whom I had invited. When the man entered the office, he had a look of grave concern on his face. He clearly thought something was wrong.

I said to this good man, "President, please relax. I just think you and I need to spend some time reviewing your responsibility as an elders quorum president. And I propose that we do so right now—while we ride together in my car to watch our sons play basketball against each other at 7:00 p.m." The man's facial expression changed from one of concern to completely amazed bewilderment! He could not imagine that his stake president was inviting him to miss a priesthood leadership meeting to watch a basketball game.

The son of the elders quorum president was playing on a team competing against my son's team in the championship game of a junior high school basketball tournament. Our drive to the site of the game would require almost two hours. We exited the building and quickly were on the way. During our ride together we had a remarkable conversation about families, work, Church service, his calling as an elders quorum president—and about junior high school basketball.

Neither the president nor I will ever forget the looks on the faces of our wives and sons as we entered the gymnasium just a few minutes before the tip-off. We shared a fun and memorable evening with our families supporting our sons.

Approximately six months later, I received an early-morning phone call from this same elders quorum president. He reported that he was at the hospital; his son, the boy who had played against my son in the basketball tournament, had been seriously injured in an accident. The president asked if I could come to the hospital. I responded that I would be there as quickly as possible.

When I walked into the emergency room, this brother greeted me with a strong embrace and tragic news. His son had died just a few minutes earlier. I was stunned to think that such an ener-getic and beloved young man suddenly was gone. I hugged that bereaved father tightly as I expressed my condolences and love. I spent precious time with my friend—both in silence and attempt-ing to provide comfort. When it seemed appropriate, I asked what had happened.

The young man had been injured in a freak accident while completing routine chores. After recounting the events that caused his son's injury and led to his subsequent passing, this dear man looked at me and said: "I am so glad we left that priesthood meeting a few months ago so we could watch our boys play in that championship game. I always will treasure the joyful memory of that night. That may have been the only chance I ever would have had to see my son play in a game like that."

Was it merely a coincidence that I had somehow felt a most unusual need to leave a Church meeting and invite an elders quo-rum president to join me? Was it a random event that this brother and I could watch our sons compete in a basketball tournament? Or was this episode divinely orchestrated by a loving Lord who knows all things, the end from the beginning, and wanted a father and a son to have a special experience together?

I believe that in the work of the Lord there is no such thing as a coincidence. And on this occasion, I was blessed to be an instru-ment through whom a tender mercy was delivered to this man and his son—because the worth of souls is great in the sight of God.

AN UNSCHEDULED MEETING WITH MISSIONARIES

While fulfilling an assignment in a foreign country, my wife, Susan, and I made an unscheduled visit to one of our missionary training centers to greet and briefly speak with approximately one hundred missionaries. Because we were en route to another appointment, we had only a short time to spend with the elders and sisters.

In my instruction to the missionaries, I described the revelatory process whereby they are called and assigned to a specific field of labor. I then explained that in the culture of the Church, we often talk of being called to serve in a country such as Argentina, Poland, Korea, or the United States. But a missionary is not called to a place; rather, he or she is called to serve. As the Lord declared to the Prophet Joseph Smith in 1829, "If ye have desires to serve God ye are called to the work" (Doctrine and Covenants 4:3).

Each mission call and assignment or later reassignment is the result of revelation through the Lord's servants. A call to the work comes from God through the President of the Church. An assignment to one of the more than four hundred missions presently operating around the world comes from God through a member of the Quorum of the Twelve Apostles, who acts with the authorization of the Lord's living prophet. The spiritual gifts of prophecy and revelation attend all mission calls and assignments.

The spiritual pattern of *one by one* is used by the Brethren as assignments or reassignments are made. Each prospective missionary is considered and assigned individually; there are no group or mass allocations of missionaries to the many missions located around the world.

I read with the missionaries section 80 of the Doctrine and Covenants, a record of a mission call to Stephen Burnett extended by the Prophet Joseph Smith in 1832. Studying this call to Brother Burnett can help us to (1) understand more clearly the distinction between being "called to the work" as a missionary and "assigned to labor" in a place and (2) appreciate more completely our individual and divinely appointed responsibility to proclaim the gospel.

Verse one of this section is a call to serve: "Verily, thus saith the Lord unto you my servant Stephen Burnett: Go ye, go ye into the world and preach the gospel to every creature that cometh under the sound of your voice."

Interestingly, verse two informs Brother Burnett about his assigned missionary companion: "And inasmuch as you desire a companion, I will give unto you my servant Eden Smith."

Verse three indicates where these two missionaries are to labor: "Wherefore, go ye and preach my gospel, whether to the north or to the south, to the east or to the west, it mattereth not, for ye cannot go amiss."

I do not believe the phrase "it mattereth not," as used by the Lord in this scripture, suggests that He does not care where His servants labor. In fact, He cares deeply. But because the work of preaching the gospel is the Lord's work, He inspires, guides, and directs His authorized servants. As missionaries strive to be ever more worthy and capable instruments in His hands and do their best to fulfill faithfully their duties, then with His help they "cannot go amiss." Perhaps one of the lessons the Savior is teaching us in this revelation is that an assignment to labor in a specific place is essential and important but secondary to the call to serve.

The next verse highlights important qualifications for all missionaries: "Therefore, declare the things which ye have *heard,* and verily *believe,* and *know to be true.*"

The final verse reminds Brother Burnett and all of us from Whom a call to serve truly comes: "Behold, this is the will of him who hath called you, your Redeemer, even Jesus Christ. Amen."

My experience has taught me that these principles are not well understood by many members of the Church. Thus, I felt a need to use our brief time with the missionaries to reiterate and emphasize these simple truths.

The single greatest reason for addressing this matter was what I have learned over time about the concern, worry, and even guilt felt by many missionaries who for various reasons were reassigned to a different field of labor during their time of service. Such reassignments sometimes are necessary because of events and circumstances such as physical accidents and injuries, delays and challenges in obtaining visas, political instability, creating and staffing new missions, or the evolving and ever-changing needs around the world in the work of proclaiming the gospel.

When a missionary is reassigned to a different field of labor, the process is precisely the same as for the initial assignment. Members of the Quorum of the Twelve seek inspiration and guidance in making all such reassignments—*one by one.*

I recounted to the missionaries a conversation I had with a faithful man who shared with me the deepest feelings of his heart after he heard me explain the difference between being called to the work and assigned to labor. This good brother shook my hand and with tears in his eyes said to me, "The things you helped me learn today have lifted a burden from my shoulders that I have carried for more than thirty years. As a young missionary, my initial assignment was to a field of labor in South America. But I was unable to obtain a visa, so my assignment was changed to the United States. All these years I have wondered why I was unable to serve in the place to which I had been called. Now I know I was called to the work and not to a place. I cannot tell you how much this understanding has helped me."

I shared with the missionaries that for the members of the Twelve, nothing affirms the reality of ongoing latter-day revelation more powerfully than seeking to discern the Lord's will as we fulfill our responsibility to assign missionaries to their respective fields of labor. I also bore my witness that the Savior knows and is mindful of each of us *one by one* and name by name.

Susan and I expressed our love to the missionaries and departed for our next appointment. As we were walking out, I whispered to Susan that I had no idea why I had used the short amount of time in this unscheduled visit to address the subject of mission calls and assignments with this particular group of missionaries. I simply believed the elders and sisters would benefit from such an explanation by a member of the Twelve.

As we neared the exit of the building, the president of the missionary training center asked if someone had informed me about the challenges confronting one of the sister missionaries. I answered that no one had told me anything about any of the sister missionaries. He then said to me with great emotion, "Elder Bednar, a sister sitting on the front row had her mission assignment changed three days ago. She has been struggling to understand why her mission call would be altered. I watched her face as you were teaching, and I believe she received the answer she needed."

I asked the mission president to accompany me, and we returned to the room where the missionaries were assembled. He identified the sister missionary, and I spent a few minutes talking with her. We discussed her concerns, and I asked if she better understood how and why the assignment had been changed. I shook the sister's hand and bore my testimony that the Lord knew her by name, as an individual, as a *one*. It was a spiritually sweet moment for both of us.

Was it merely a coincidence that Susan and I adjusted our itinerary and schedule so we could meet with the missionaries? Was it a random event that I described the process whereby mission calls and assignments are made? Or was this episode divinely orchestrated by a loving Lord who knew and responded to the concerns of a young sister missionary—a *one?*

I believe that in the work of the Lord there is no such thing as a coincidence. And on this occasion, I was blessed to be an instrument through whom a tender mercy was delivered to this young woman—because the worth of souls is great in the sight of God.

I repeat again for emphasis: the Savior cannot send General Authorities, general auxiliary leaders, stake presidents, bishops, Relief Society presidents, and other auxiliary leaders to minister single-handedly to the needs of every member in all units of His restored Church. I do not know why some individuals, such as the sister missionary in the episode I just described, receive blessings and learn a lesson through the ministry of a general Church leader while others receive similar blessings and learn lessons in alternative and equally effective ways. I do not know all of the reasons, all of the purposes, and I do not know everything about the Lord's timing. With Nephi, you and I can say that we "do not know the meaning of all things" (1 Nephi 11:17).

But some things I absolutely do know. I know the Lord tailors our tutorials to our individual needs, capacity, and circumstances. I know He knows us by name and as *ones.* And I know the Savior bestows upon us His tender mercies and bounteous blessings using whatever means best accomplish His purposes and facilitate our individual spiritual growth.

A HEARTFELT QUESTION

Many years ago, Susan and I met with a large congregation of youth between the ages of twelve and eighteen in a Latin American country. I invited the young people to ask gospel questions, and we did our best to respond to their inquiries.

As the meeting was about to conclude, I called upon a young boy seated on the front row of the chapel to pose his question. He stood and simply asked, "How can I learn to be successful at anything in my life?" I have never forgotten this boy's question and the way it was asked. There was a sincerity, an earnestness, a desire, and a pleading in this young man's eyes and voice that penetrated my heart. I felt an instant and overpowering love for him. I attempted to answer his question by explaining basic gospel principles that would surely bless him—in his youth and through-out his life. We answered a few additional questions and then concluded the meeting.

During the singing of the closing hymn, I asked one of the priesthood leaders on the stand to please invite the young boy who had asked about becoming successful to meet with me for a few minutes. Susan and I shook hands with many of the young people, and then we exited the chapel and began walking toward an exit into the parking lot.

The boy was waiting for me near the exit, and, as I ap-proached, he ran and fell into my arms. We embraced and, with the assistance of a translator, talked for a few minutes about what he had learned in the question-and-answer session. As we finished our conversation, I gave him a card with my contact information and invited him to write me letters periodically. I encouraged him to stay in touch with me and indicated that I was interested in knowing how he was doing in school and in his preparation to receive the Melchizedek Priesthood.

Over the years this boy developed into a young man, and he kept his promise to send me updates several times a year. I was especially pleased to learn about his desire to live righteously and to be worthy of priesthood and temple blessings. He looked forward with great anticipation to serving as a full-time missionary.

Approximately five years after I first met this boy, I was working in Salt Lake City assigning missionaries to their respective fields of labor. As I recall, for that specific week I had a group of approximately 250 elders and sisters to be assigned. Imagine my delight and wonder, as I was working to fulfill my responsibility, to learn that this young man was among the prospective missionaries I was to assign. Our communication over the years had provided me with specific insights about his desires, preparation, background, and capabilities. I felt the Spirit guide my thinking and confirm the correctness of the assignment he received. It was a remarkable and heaven-facilitated experience.

Was it merely a coincidence that I became acquainted and corresponded with this young man over a period of many years? Was it a random event that he was included in a group of missionaries for me to assign? Or were these episodes divinely orchestrated by a loving Lord who knew the needs and potential of a young missionary—a *one?*

I believe that in the work of the Lord there is no such thing as a coincidence. And on this occasion, I was blessed to be simultaneously the recipient of a tender mercy and an instrument through whom a tender mercy was delivered to this young man—because the worth of souls is great in the sight of God.

TRAGEDY ON A UNIVERSITY CAMPUS

On April 16, 2007, a student shot and killed thirty-two people and wounded seventeen others in two separate attacks on the campus of Virginia Tech University in Blacksburg, Virginia. The incident was one of the deadliest shooting rampages in American history.

The shootings occurred on a Monday. I was assigned to be in Blacksburg the following Saturday and Sunday to preside at a stake conference. After learning about the horrific event, I recorded the following entry in my journal: "Interestingly, I am scheduled for a weekend conference in that very stake this coming weekend. . . . It will be for me a 'tender mercy' to visit the campus and the stake and to bring the authority of the apostleship to an area that needs spiritual assurance and succor."

My companion for the weekend assignment, Elder Anthony

Burns, and I were blessed to meet Saturday morning with students, faculty members, employees, and other people who were affected by the tragedy. We discussed why sometimes bad things happen to good people, answered questions, and bore witness of the Eternal Father's plan of salvation, of the living reality of the Savior, and of the Lord's power to calm, comfort, and strengthen us.

Elder Burns and I walked with the stake president around portions of the campus and across a large drill field. The windows on the second floor of Norris Hall through which students during the attack had jumped to safety were still broken out and open. Privately a prayer was offered and a blessing invoked that peace might be received by all who were adversely impacted by the assault, that healing might occur, and that a spirit of restoration and recovery would brood over Blacksburg and the campus and facilitate a return to normalcy more rapidly than might otherwise be anticipated.

Was it merely a coincidence that a member of the Quorum of the Twelve had been assigned many months earlier to preside at a stake conference in Blacksburg, Virginia, only days after such a horrendous event? Was it a random occurrence that an authorized servant of the Lord was in a place with people who needed blessings, solace, and comfort? Or were these episodes divinely orchestrated by a loving Lord who knew the distress of victims and the unsettledness of a community?

I believe that in the work of the Lord there is no such thing as a coincidence. And on this occasion, my companion and I were blessed to deliver tender mercies to many individuals—because the worth of souls is great in the sight of God.

A YOUNG WOMAN'S FAITH AND SACRIFICE

On an assignment in a foreign country, Susan and I were blessed to participate in an evening devotional with a large group of young single adults. The meeting began at 7:00 p.m. and was held in a stake center in a large city. I invited the young people to ask questions, and we enjoyed a memorable evening interacting with these future husbands and wives, fathers and mothers, and leaders of the Church and of their communities.

I was especially impressed by a young woman who posed a question near the end of the meeting. She was sitting on the front row of the chapel next to the exit door to my right. Her question was spiritually mature, insightful, thoughtful, and focused upon a topic that required great courage to articulate in a large congregation. The substance and tone of her inquiry invited a particularly sweet spirit into the gathering.

Before attempting to answer, I commended her for the quality of her preparation to ask such an inspired question. Following my response and a final testimony, we sang the closing hymn and concluded the meeting with a benediction. We shook hands with the young people, and I sought out the young woman and again thanked her for her inspired contribution to the meeting. We then returned to our hotel.

One of the local stake presidents accompanied us during the drive to our accommodations. He asked me if I knew anything about the young woman whom I had invited to ask the final question in the devotional. I indicated that I did not know her or anything about her.

The stake president had noticed the young woman earlier in the day as he was checking on the sound system in the building and making other preparations for the devotional. He talked with her and learned about her background, her faith, and the sacrifices she had made to attend the meeting. The president reported that she had traveled approximately eight hours on a bus from a distant city to be there. The cost of the ticket for her journey was significant, but she was extremely excited to gather with other young adults for a special occasion. She had arrived at the main bus station in the city in the early afternoon and walked many miles to the stake center, then waited patiently in the chapel for several hours prior to the meeting.

The president then observed, "I believe it was a tender mercy of the Lord that you invited that young woman to ask the final question of the evening. The opportunity for a sister from such a remote area to talk with a member of the Twelve about an important subject was a blessing in her life."

Was it merely a coincidence that this young woman was

invited to ask the final question in that young single adult devotional? Was it a random event that the stake president rode with us to the hotel and could inform me about her great faith in the Savior and the sacrifices she had made in order to attend the meeting? Or were these episodes divinely orchestrated by a loving Lord who acknowledged the remarkable devotion of a faithful young sister—a *one?*

I believe that in the work of the Lord there is no such thing as a coincidence. And on this occasion, I was blessed to deliver a tender mercy to this young woman—because the worth of souls is great in the sight of God.

SUMMARY

The examples described in this chapter can help us recognize how tender mercies many times are delivered to an individual by another person—*one by one.* A latter-day hymn emphasizes the role of ordinary people doing seemingly ordinary things that are important in accomplishing God's purposes.

You can make the pathway bright,
Fill the soul with heaven's light,
If there's sunshine in your heart;
Turning darkness into day,
As the shadows fly away,
If there's sunshine in your heart today.

You can speak the gentle word
  To the heart with anger stirred,
If there's sunshine in your heart;
  Tho it seems a little thing,
It will heaven's blessings bring,
  If there's sunshine in your heart today.

You can do a kindly deed
  To your neighbor in his need,
If there's sunshine in your heart;
  And his burden you will share
As you lift his load of care,
  If there's sunshine in your heart today.

You can live a happy life
  In this world of toil and strife,
If there's sunshine in your heart;
  And your soul will glow with love
From the perfect Light above,
  If there's sunshine in your heart today.
  (Hymns [1985], no. 228)

A book about the Savior's spiritual pattern of ministering *one by one* ultimately can never be completed. Such a book has no final summary or concluding chapter. Rather, it should contain a never-ending series of episodes and experiences focusing upon individuals. The book finally will be finished when "the purposes of God shall be accomplished, and the Great Jehovah shall say the work is done" (*History of the Church,* 4:540).

Each of us as a disciple of the Lord still has many additional chapters to write in our own personal book of experiences with the principle of *one by one.* As we consistently seek for eyes to see and ears to hear, we can discern and detect the tender mercies of the Lord in our lives—as we are blessed both to receive them and to act as instruments in the hands of the Savior to deliver them to other people.

Withhold not thou thy *tender mercies* from me, O Lord: let thy lovingkindness and thy truth continually preserve me. (Psalm 40:11)

Let thy *tender mercies* come unto me, that I may live: for thy law is my delight. (Psalm 119:77)

Great are thy *tender mercies,* O Lord: quicken me according to thy judgments. (Psalm 119:156)

The Lord is good to all: and his *tender mercies* are over all his works. (Psalm 145:9)

And they did land upon the shore of the promised land. And when they had set their feet upon the shores of the promised land they bowed themselves down upon the face of the land, and did humble themselves before the Lord, and did shed tears of joy before the Lord, because of the multitude of his *tender mercies* over them. (Ether 6:12)

I joyfully testify that God lives and is our Heavenly Father. He is the author of the plan of salvation. Jesus is the Christ, the Redeemer, whose body was bruised, broken, and torn for us as He offered the atoning sacrifice. He is resurrected, He lives, and He stands at the head of His Church in these latter days. To be "encircled about eternally in the arms of his love" (2 Nephi 1:15) will be a real and not a virtual experience.

On a future day, every knee shall bow and every tongue confess that Jesus is the Christ. And on that blessed day, we will know He knows each of us by name. He knows each of us as a *one*— because the worth of souls is great in the sight of God.

Questions to Consider

1. What can and should I do to learn to recognize and acknowledge appropriately the Lord's hand in all things?

2. How does increasing my understanding of the tender mercies of the Lord and the work of the ministry affect my motives, my heart, and my behavior?

3. What can and should I do to more fully believe that both the tender mercies of the Lord and the spiritual pattern of ministering *one by one* apply personally in my life?

My Own Questions to Consider

1. _____
   _____

2. _____
   _____

3. _____
   _____

Scriptures Related to What I Am Learning

_____

_____

_____

INDEX